HAMMER
OF THE GODS

Hammer Of The Gods
Selected writings by
Friedrich Nietzsche
A Creation Book
Compiled, edited & translated by:
Stephen Metcalf
ISBN 1 871592 46 1
First published 1996 by:
Creation Books
London
Reprinted 1996, 1997, 1998, 1999
© Copyright Stephen Metcalf 1995
This edition © Copyright Creation Books 1996
All rights reserved

CONTENTS

REFERENCE CODES

Translations are based on the Giorgio Colli and Mazzino Montinari (editors) edition of Nietzsche's *Werke* (Walter de Gruyter & Co., Berlin, 1969), the titles of which are abbreviated throughout this selection as follows:

BT	*The Birth Of Tragedy* (1871)
HH	*Human, All-Too Human* (1878)
WS	*The Wanderer And His Shadow* (1879)
D	*Daybreak* (1880)
GS	*The Gay Science* (1882)
Z	*Thus Spoke Zarathustra* (1883-85)
BGE	*Beyond Good And Evil* (1886)
GM	*On The Genealogy Of Morals* (1887)
TI	*The Twilight Of The Idols* (1888)
A	*The Antichrist* (1888)
DD	*Dionysus Dithyrambs* (1888)
EH	*Ecce Homo* (1888)
PF	Posthumously published fragments and notebooks (1880s)
L	Letters
S	Arthur Schopenhauer – *Philosophical Writings* (Ed. Wolfgang Schirmacher, Continuum, N.Y., 1994)

INTRODUCTION

"EVEN WHEN THE HEART BLEEDS"

1. DEAD GOD.

A cold wind blows across empty space. Dark matter obscures
the sun. Wreckage of exploded stars drifts in the void, the
ruins of a solar system, burned-out at 3,000K, radiating
annihilation in all directions. A single beam of light, cutting
through the gloom, frames the silhouetted body of a dead God,
stretching cruciform across the galaxy; face taut with pain,
spikes wounding wrist and ankle – borne continually upwards
towards the vault of the Heavens, where divinities go to die,
but all the while drawn down into the abyss below. Lead
weights lashed to the base and the vertical struts of the scaffold
plumb the deep. The crucified hangs on a counterweight,
falling far into emptiness. While He thirsts for eternal order,
purity, light, redemption, the counterweight pulls all that is
holy back down towards the distant memory of something
darker: the general economy of base matter, meat, blood, and
blind impulse from which it was emitted – a mistake dropping
off the end of a human production line. A human product
which suddenly reaches the scrap heap of worthless ideas in

an unplanned obsolescence. Dead God. Aborted divinity. Enemy of multitude stars. Stone baby of the macrocosm. Evacuated cyclopean eye of the celestial sphere.

Shadows black-out the horizon in a single stroke. Morbid expectations of apocalypse. Ledgers kept in minute detail plot the geometries and timescales of the end of the world. Vertigo and nausea proliferate, requiring that the stomach expands to accommodate ever greater magnitudes of sickness. Pulsing chaos tears apart the fabric of the universe. The last days fade out along the line of a fuse....

So what was it that ruined this passional gothic theatre of obliteration? What was it that robbed us of the comic spectacle of all the sinners falling to their knees, hands outstretched in terror, before all being wiped-out in some final holocaust of divine judgement? It was this: *something like divine order without God.* God's shadow, smeared on the walls of his burial cave. Transcendental authority.

Deicide undertaken, and the old Logos of the universe a bloodless corpse, hacked into pieces by a multitude of blades; business confidence is not shaken at all along a street of graves, churches, memorials, tombs. In fact, something of an upturn is taking place. No-one is troubled by the sound of gravediggers echoing across the marketplace at daybreak. No-one detects the faint smell of death which hangs in the mist. And this is why: by itself, the death of God is not a particularly significant event – we have no interest in repeatedly exhuming the sacred corpse in order to cut it down again, however gratifying the feeling of revenge might be.

We mistrust the death of this God. And if our decadent fantasies should once again turn towards this theological apocalypse which failed to complete itself, and trickled away into inexistence, are we not, then, merely longing for His second coming? Do we have to condemn ourselves to eternal nostalgia for the intransitory?

To us, the death of God is a cipher; a slash of shorthand marking the absence of any stable centre to the universe – the desolation of any spike on which the celestial sphere rotates, impaled, like a worn-out gyroscope running down to a halt. And the celestial sphere itself.

After all, God was one of our more benign errors. We can only speculate as to how comforting the idea of Him can have been for childlike monotheistic savages – people who needed the preternatural apparition of some old patriarch, stroking his long, grey beard somewhere up in the stratosphere, in order to drift out into exhausted hibernation: who needed someone who added purpose to life, encrypting an originary guilt-trip upon an organism coming into being by projecting its utter self-loathing back at itself from a geographically infinite, ethereal domain beyond the earth.

One huge Copernican revolution later (that of Kant), this guilty catholic promise of no future energizes the economy as protestant liberalism translates the realm of debt onto the commodity form and its potentially endless circulation. An anthropomorphized universe grinds into slow revolutions around Man, humanity, human laws; reason which dictates its concepts, axioms, numbers, bodies, planes, causes, and effects to the universe. Order is maintained, without any interruption from God, by means of pain machines, contracts, tribunals, legal systems, communities, cultures, states – subjects and authors: beings, all *a priori* legally responsible for their own actions – teleologically judging themselves to be the ultimate end of evolution. The ultimate man. The last man.

This is why the death of God is so insignificant. Humanism's project – to set the value of everything in place by processing it all through this secular digestive system – looms out of the chaotic manifold of deep space as an infinitely more functional machine for the maintenance of cosmic order than feeble theology ever was. It seals itself off from the future where it falls down ruined. Maybe this is the last and greatest revenge of religious souls stripped of their divinity. For what does it make of anyone seeking to think beyond these structures? Illegitimate, insane, illegal, inhuman, impossible. A dead fanatic – something that squanders its life howling mad curses in semi-silenced desperation.

Beyond the shorelines of this temperate cultural belt, there is only the jungle, where animal eyes glower, yellow, with hunger and malice; the scorched, white expanses of the desert, or the metallic water tables of the steppes and the tundra; the violent turbulence of the ocean, churning storm fronts, and hurricanes. Everything is at sea, the gaze perhaps turning back towards the safety of all that lies behind. We turn to the south, where we will melt in futuristic heat.

2.   THE ECSTASY OF THE TRAGIC/SELF-OVERCOMING.
Lighting lanterns against a sky washed orange by a new dawn, the blood of God fresh on our hands, breath coming in hoarse gasps, no longer ourselves, we begin to unpick the locks holding a gate marked 'Catastrophe' shut. Slipping all moorings and venturing out onto oceans of virtual death, standing once again in the foaming surf, breakers lapping around our feet, trembling in restless ecstasy, we are gradually inserted into a labyrinth, a complex of little alleys and corridors, flattened into an infernal gaming table and marked with the name 'Nietzsche'. Perhaps we have been here before. How easily we forget.

The labyrinth of existence possesses an end, some kind of goal towards which life impetuously rushes (but never *the* end). At the same time, it is plastic, mutable, and constantly shifting ground – such that there is no predetermined map, no territorial imperative, no transcendental domain attainable from which to assault the material singularities of over- abundant existence. Drunk on the narcotic pessimism of Schopenhauer and Wagner, Nietzsche botched this insight in "The Birth Of Tragedy" – in seeking to resolve the periodic, chaotic, tendency to subjective dissolution in orgiastic festivals of self-destruction, by means of mediating between two transcendental principles of homeostasis, marked with the names of Greek deities: Apollonian and Dionysian. Dream and intoxication. The capture of intense experience in images. These two principles came together on the stage of Greek tragedy (or, in a point that would later make Nietzsche so nauseous, in the total art of Richard Wagner), where fatalism runs along the line of a pre-established, irreversible chain of events, according to a divine project unknown to its victim; where the inner combustion of Dionysian ecstasy always ends up governed by Apollonian moderation. Transcendence has its foundations shaken, as the *principium individuationis* threatens to fall apart, but never fully collapses. Suffering, pain, and ecstasy swim in superficial seas – formed out of the accumulation of centuries of poetic dribbling. The infantile laments of born failures contain the Dionysian refrain; dazzled in the footlights, stagestruck, and drowned out in a cacophony where the voice captures the intensity of the dance.

Nietzsche's later thought cuts the thought of the tragic/fatal loose from this idealist, representational grid. Tragedy hardwired to the transhistorical is flattened-out into a continual play of chance and necessity: necessity which does not entail the abolition of chance; necessity which becomes fatal when the dice thrown out against the future return to reveal their outcome – the singular number that is no other, at once irreplaceable and multiple – coupled to a recurring innocence that continually wipes the slate of existence clean and affirms this drawing of lots (*Loos* = fate, destiny), even if the outcome is detrimental. Nietzsche's love for the philosophers of the future capable of gambling thus is profound; they know how to probe their depths, they have learned to love the results of this reckless experiment, "they admit to finding pleasure in the acts of negation and dissection, and to a kind of self-possessed cruelty which knows how to wield the knife with certainty and mastery even when the heart bleeds." [BGE]

Philosophers of the future ride currents of fatal multiplicity into an intensified, unresolved, uncertain climate – something like a new zone in the tropics – possessing no higher dimensions than those of its own flat, multiple field. God is dead, and any theory which preaches the attainment of any afterlife – a numbing, deathlike paradise out of this world – judges against life and contaminates it with the bacillus of revenge, responsibility, guilt.

In the labyrinth, the self-possessed individual suffers the same bodily dismemberment as Dionysus (the singular name now marking the spacetime of the tragic) in order to attain its multiple phase shifts – which lock onto courses stripped of any notion of personal responsibility. The enemy is no longer ecstasy but redemption: all that scans the distance for a way out of the labyrinth. Dionysus goes to war with Christ, and life becomes a matter of navigating the labyrinth and all the minotaurs, bloodshed, and cremation it entails. "Life itself, its eternal fruitfulness and recurrence, is a matter of agony, destruction, the will to annihilation." [PF]

In order to overcome the potentially suicidal lure of a life stripped of purpose, Nietzsche no longer bets on the laws of thermodynamics which guarantee that energy will run down to the indifferent terminus of an equilibrium of forces. And neither does he attempt to heal all of life's wounds, boredom, and pain (as Schopenhauer did) by means of a recourse to hope and pity – neither of which will compensate for a life of suffering since "the course of a man's life is, as a rule, such that, having been duped by hope, he dances into the arms of death." [S] But all this is imaginary, an idea, all this hope, all this self-pity: life grasped as a beachhead in a storm, lashed by the savagery of the ocean, with only the self-deluded, brattish suffering of bourgeois poets for protection, wailing at the cyclone for calm and order. Suffering with nothing palpable to overcome; romanticism, and pallid decadence. Tears and purple flowers scattered on the graves of youth's murdered dreams. The tragic beauty of the exhumed corpse of that revolting plethora of sentiment, poetry.

It is at this point that Nietzsche's thought turns towards the question of the exercise of the will; a philosophy initially issuing from the pessimistic climatological zone delineated by Schopenhauer where "the will, considered purely in itself, is entirely devoid of knowledge; it is only a blind, irresistible urge, as we see it appear in inorganic and vegetable nature and in their laws, and also in the vegetative part of our own life." [S] It is pure impulse, force, and not a political organization bent on the enslavement of all society under a dictatorship (as the most common and cretinous misreading of Nietzsche would have it). Nietzsche's main move beyond Schopenhauer is to cease to view the will as an object of revulsion, energizing a feeling of horror and pity at all that has been condemned to live, organically bind itself together, and reproduce (the will to live).

Transvalued by Nietzsche, the primal will functions as an impulse for power – an essentially plastic, mutable, brutally materialist conception of a simultaneously motive and formative power, which synthesizes modes of evaluation – enmeshing the will to live within itself. The will to power never overdetermines all that which it synthesizes. It operates on a plane of immanence which is never higher or wider than its field of application (all that which it operates upon). It metamorphoses itself, slipping into every skin, always within this labyrinthine field; determining itself along with all that it determines. It is completely irresponsible, a source of energy, the genesis of all actions, feelings, and thoughts. As raw impulsive force, it constantly exceeds the goals and targets set by whoever or whatever evaluates and synthesizes by means of it: it is always already modifying this goal and target, cutting away at the foundations of any continuous identity intended for it – the dissonance of the suicidal being dissolved in the consonant synthesis of the Eternal Return where past, present, and future converge and the individual will is abolished.

Nietzsche is a catastrophe theorist; which is to say that processes of synthesis and evaluation do not run down towards somnambulant equilibrium. They tend towards critical points – phase shifts – where the thick black ice holding the present fixed in place, the terminator on the surface of the planet marking the sunlit zones of enlightenment off from their dark areas, becomes fluid once more. Where the fixed zero degree of the Celsius scale is blasted by a solar wind howling across interplanetary space. Hammers crashing against prison walls of values held at equilibrated ice point, the hibernators awaken to throw evaluation back into streams of becoming. Gravothermal collapse hurls the fixed stars out of their cyclic orbits. Immense galaxies open up on the dark side, beyond the line of the terminator, turning towards the chaotic manifold with a burst of belly laughter which counterweights the will to annihilation: "Those were just steps for me. I have now climbed on over them. Therefore I must have journeyed beyond them. But you thought I wanted to sit upon them and rest." [PF] Humanity continually goes over and across towards its own overcoming. The technics of its bridge-building ensures this. Nothing can preserve it from this catastrophe.

To trace the various speeds and velocities of this process, Nietzsche's method is to relate any concept coming under experimental scrutiny to the will to power and ask: who is it that wills this? What kind of drive reaches out to evaluate like this? From what mode of evaluation does this will radiate? And not just who wants power (quantitative question), but what kind of power (qualitative question)? Is it masterful, active, self-affirming, and tragic (i.e. fatal)? – or slavish, negative, and dialectical (as we shall see later): the will to the end?

Countless luminous globes orbit in endless space, around which revolve a series of smaller, illuminated bodies – hot at the core and covered with a cold crust, over which a mouldy film is spread: the world, the real – ideas in the mind burning their imaginary laws onto the body of the earth, the movements of the stars, the dissipating heat of the sun.

In the quaint nomenclature of 18th century astrophysics, 'fixed' stars hung like baubles in the night sky. Truth lay striated on the 'fact' that they did not alter their position in the celestial sphere, relative to the earthbound observer. Such stars acquired this name as a means of distinguishing them from 'wandering' stars; stars which were permitted to move by the postulates of scientific reason – the planets. But the appearance of fixity is only a matter of *distance*. (Sometimes things which appear to be close lie at an imperceptible point in the distance). Stars which lie far beyond our insignificant solar system appeared to be fixed in place owing to the tremendous stretch of time necessary for their light to become perceptible. The light source did not seem to alter. A little more enlightenment and the scientific guardians of "natural" law know what has really been going on: they discover the 'proper motion' of stars across the celestial sphere – a little changeling imagining the earth and the observer to be at the centre of a sphere within which the positions of celestial bodies are plotted for the purpose of calculating the distance between them. Nothing moves. Nothing changes. Whoever thought that the earth orbits the sun? The thought of fixity is suddenly annulled in the "knowledge" of movement. After one of these catastrophes, the past can be accessed and transvalued – for wasn't this *always* so? Coming out of the neotropic hot zone of phase space, is it not true that one merely lives before or after these events? (But still, news of the event takes so much time to arrive. The shadows still need to be erased from the wall.)

And so it is with humanity. The human already contains the principle of some kind of evolution beyond itself, the germ of some future mutation, the technics to peel off all second skins. To the best of our scientific knowledge, the nature of humanity may appear to be *fixed in place* – when measured against a false linear, teleological calculus which freezes over becoming in being. It is a question of *faith*, faith in science, faith in God, faith in humanity, which orders the universe *as if* all this were true now and eternally – a permanent Copernican revolution coating the horrifying apprehension of universal disorder in layer upon layer of human ideas which dictate their laws to nature: human, microcosmic meaning raised to the macrocosm. (For the slaves: telos, paradise. For the masters: terminus, death.) "We hold unities to be necessary, in order to calculate: but that is not to accept that such unities actually exist. We have balanced the concept of unity upon our concept of "I" – our oldest article of faith." [PF]

Nietzsche's materialism reinvests calculus with chaos – counter-revolutionizing the Copernican universe with ruthless, dehumanized, heliocentric fatalism which cuts away at the theologically sedimented bedrock of the transcendental subject. In this over-abundant economy of active, solar excess nothing is to be held accountable for itself in the general malaise of chaos, chance, and transvaluation – all of which strips the world of its thin, fragile, pessimistic shell and plunges it into ever more profound depths of the impersonal: *the inhuman.* This solar force is the energy enabling all undertakings, not the desired effect that prompts the cause of that effect by means of a reverse inference from the product to the idea that produced it. In the laboratory of this general economy of squandered wealth, reaching out beyond itself towards the unattainable goal of the Overman (unattainable because to think otherwise would be to suppose a final destination): "Humanity is really more of a means than an end. Humanity is merely experimental material, the monstrous surplus of bad breeding, a pile of rubble." [PF] Material which lives dangerously, in the pursuit of yet more experiments.

3. THE WILL TO THE END/ON THE ART OF DYING/THE THIRST FOR REVENGE/THE NEW IDOL.

It is here that Nietzsche's vivisection of humanity is driven towards the black hole at the source of Western modes of evaluation – radiating pessimism in all directions, sucking all matter and energy into its nihilistic core. Everywhere, throughout the course of the last 2,000 years, the active mode of evaluation (the will that constantly goes into combat with its own highest achievements) has been crushed in the dense mass of reactive force – suicidally seductive black body radiation: the will that fixes everything in place, and wants the end.

Too feeble to stand on its own terms, the will to the end is not destined to triumph as a superior force. Reactive force only ever fights back *against active force* – evaluating it out of existence in terms of its manifest image in the mirror of some tangle of reactive forces. It restricts, limits, and negates – and only then, after this arduous work of negation, does it find a substratum of strength available to it to affirm itself (always in terms of what it is not). Inversion of the evaluating eye where, increasingly, nobility, the abundant largesse of active force, can only see itself reflected in the specular regime of the Chandala. The jaundiced eye overcodes all the other organs. A trap which lures the masters into the grey, negative mesh of an anorexic economy which constitutes itself by externalizing its self-loathing – ascetic ideals, guilt, bad conscience, and ressentiment (the thirst for revenge). This point informs all of Nietzsche's critique of Darwinism, since "it has always been necessary to protect the strong from the weak." [PF] The dialectical mechanisms of Christianity, all the masks of its self-hate, enable the slaves to defeat the masters, maintain socio-political domination, and profit from the emergent bourgeois economy – while always remaining slaves.

Revenge and reaction, retaliation drawn out across millennia and cloaked in egalitarian sentiments like "love" and "justice", reverse all noble values in initiating an equalization process; the will to "breed an animal with the right to make promises." [GM] A creature which remains faithful to its obligations, with or without the intervention of God: a creature that understands that if it breaks its promises, it will face all the painful consequences of its treason. In this, its creative, revolutionary phase; slave morality calculates by means of subsuming all economic exchange under the mercantile contractual relationship between creditor and debtor. Everything has its equivalent. Everything can be paid for. Somehow, everything will be paid for.

What follows is a wholesale carve-up of the body – its organs all plugged into primitive machineries of cruelty, the pain machine, which codes and legislates the relative value of the various body parts in an economics of amputation. Both creditor and debtor are swallowed by an immense digestive system which marks the body according to the postulates of a regime constituting the organism as such – (i.e. as a despotism governed by the bad conscience/consciousness of reactive modes of evaluation) – and its insertion into the community. Organs energized by their coupling to the pain machine have a memory constituted for them, a memory burned into all the circuits of the organism – which still strains towards the terminal state where all process and becoming end – *once and for all.* Perpetual present and paradise which only thinks of its past agony as a reference outside itself. You will suffer: not for what you might do in the future, but for what you did in the past; all by means of this formula: injury done = pain to be suffered. Revenge as "justice", as "good" – tarantula venom washed around the mouths of "virtuous" (which is to say: functional) members of the community.

With a few basic ideas rendered inextinguishable by means of their coupling to ascetic mnemotechnics of sacrifice before the threat of pain – guaranteed by the twin hydra heads of religion and the state – all that which cements the community together in glacial inertia guarantees the initiation of an entropic process of degeneration. The will to power declines in that it is no longer capable of waging wars against its own highest achievements, it no longer drives itself out beyond itself, and is content to light fires in the cold of morning to comfort itself in the darkness of its ice age. It rests in escalating stupidity, in *decadence*, in passive nihilism.

Assuming that nothing new is possible, the looming, shadowy mechanisms of the pain machine covering all the exits from the community, the despotic regime of equals; reactive force results in a complex security system, policing itself from top to bottom (from the state down to the individuated being). Equalization processes operate as an apparatus of capture, drawing everything towards its insertion into this communitarian body as an expedient organ. With everything attracted towards this black hole and expressed, analysed, and judged in terms of interlocking gridworks of reactive forces, one would not delude oneself too far in noticing something of the exhumed remains of God guaranteeing this transcendental authority – an atheistic religion for the necromancers of the modern age: the authoritarian backwash behind all questioning; the face of God on the white wall, the effigy of Christ on the deathshroud, the theological grammar attesting to the sanctity of being, Ariadne's incessant demands for recognition – her matriarchal body administering the passage out of life by means of a silver thread. (She kisses her seal on the underworld. Old mother death).

Even the Overman, the emergent heuristic dream of active forces, hatches out of the rotten yolk of a basilisk's egg – sparkling tears from Heaven dissolving the afterbirth – as the maggot man, the ultimate pale, ill-constituted, decadent failure, learns to croak a few of Nietzsche's hook lines as founding dogmas of the Thousand Year Reich. The European cesspool echoes with the fearful, ridiculous cry of this limitless, reactive, nationalistic killing spree: "long live death!" – in the ruins where murder and suicide swirl together in a vortex of nihilism.

The state outlaws all active force that cannot be merged with its military pain machines. No-one will ever be legally permitted to live by their own rules. The war machine of active force, which hurtles into combat with the evaluation and enforcement systems of the ice age, will always be equated with *evil*. But what of it? Better to die than live here! (On condition that that death is at the right time.)

In the embers of twilight, where the sun of Enlightenment, bathed in dark matter, is blotted-out in the pitch-black of empty space, the magnitude of Nietzsche's treason against the species becomes brutally apparent. *Ressentiment*, the bad conscience, nihilism, and the will to the end are not just physiological traits of some profound sickness, but the foundations of humanity in Man. Bootstrapped into existence by the turbulent irruption of Great Politics, the declaration of a nuclear war to the death against all the cellular enclaves of the organism, active force fights against the nature of humanity as such.

No longer content to feed all life into an insatiable digestive system of ideas, which judges against it by means of all the somatic tribunals of a transcendental regime and its enforcement agencies, philosophy becomes a katabolic accelerator – increasingly amnesiac with regard to all that has happened before, and learning to live for all that is yet to come – a kind of active nihilism, emerging from degeneration, bent on destroying the organic security of the present only to gamble on a plunge into the labyrinth of an incalculable future. More experiments. More living on the edge of constant danger. The philosopher as a war machine: "I sometimes think that I lead a highly dangerous life, since I am one of those machines that can fall apart." [1] But what does that biographical entity, tattooed with the patronymic "Nietzsche" matter? – except as a singular, intensive zone, drifting like a refugee through the Eternal Return, conducting a vortical flow which tears down the frosty veils of Christian morality in order to confront all the joys and horror of life head-on. The disgust you feel as you re-emerge from a general economy of base matter, stripped of its beautiful soul, subsides as your body processes the intensity and starts to *learn*. Under-standing is no longer enough.

Transvalued, the Antichrist turns to you and smiles....

4. ETERNAL RETURN.

Eternal Return – First Aspect

The swarming phase space of the Eternal Return generates the heat necessary to thaw out the winter philosophy of the cold North and its ideas of the terminal state, equilibrium, being, the end. Put simply: if the universe were to have a state of equilibrium, the end of becoming and evolution, then it would already have attained it. The present moment, the meditation at the gate marked "Now", the instant which passes away into the void of dead time, proves that it has not been attained: an equilibrium of forces will never come to pass. The infinity of the void of dead time signs the death certificate of being – since becoming cannot have started to become. It is not something that *has* become, it is the becoming *of* something – a sometimes smooth, sometimes interrupted process of becoming. Never having become, it would already *be* what it becomes if it were to become something. In other words: becoming would never have left its original state if it had one. The only stable element in becoming is recurrence – the more or less constant traits in a flow of becoming with no beginning or end. At the gate marked "Now", past, present, and future coagulate in a synthetic relation between this moment and other moments to come and be similarly squandered – an immense vortex of time dropping the Newtonian arrow into the depths of the ocean.

If the present was condemned to congeal in the frozen inertia of the anticipation of the arrival of a new present in order to pass, then the past in general would never be constituted (since the present would be left waiting at the gate for this to happen – eternally) and the present could not pass away. Impatient, unsated like flames licking at the distance, ever-hungry for new horizons, this waiting is impossible for us. The moment is simultaneously present and past, as well as present and simultaneously future in order for it to pass away in favour of other moments. Bit streams of recurrent traits synthesize complexes, marked with proper names, which doubly affirm all this passing away and becoming – the names delineating passages through the labyrinth of existence, with all its dead ends and wrong turnings.

Burning in the magenta sky above Turin, closed time like curves access intense wavelengths of becoming; influx and reflux – fluctuations in intensity, the whole of a life experienced in a day – punching in the fusing sequences of the digital logic of a temporal philosophy for time travellers, at the moment of impact when Nietzsche's brain explodes. 1888–2012: "The unending metamorphosis: in a short time-span you must pass through several individual states. Incessant war is the means." [PF]

Brain stem irradiated in the black light of an artificial sun burning on the earth, flow and flow, drifting through a complex of mobile states, becoming innumerable others, living through a series of possible selves which flit into consciousness briefly before being forgotten. I navigate the labyrinth by scratching proper names, in chalk, on the walls channelling the passage of these intensive singularities: Dionysus; Apollo; Ariadne, the nagging voice; Silenus, prophet of death; Schopenhauer, the gloomy educator; Wagner, the delusions of youth; Bonaparte, Borgia, the beasts of prey; Nietzsche; Fontenelle, the comic aphorist; Zarathustra, the avatar of the Overman; even the Crucified himself – I, I croak, what am I? "I am Prado, I am also the father of Prado. Further, I say that I am also De Lesseps. I wanted to give my beloved Parisians a new idea – the idea of a decent criminal. I am also Chambige – also a decent criminal.... The worst thing, the thing that really nags at my modesty, is that, at base, *every name in history is I.*" [L]

Eternal Return – Second Aspect

The demon that creeps into your solitude, that follows you even into the subterranean caverns of your nightmares, plants a rule there. Act with a degree of caution: whatever you will recurs eternally. This is what initially causes the demon to appear as a malign spirit, and a surging wave of panic and nausea to rock you to the core at the thought of the Eternal Return. Calculating the nature of humanity in a register of *ressentiment*, guilt, and decadence forces you to search for the answer to a question uneasily squirming in the hive of your mind: how can the nihilistic will, the will that wants the end, affirm its own passing and becoming?

Dogs howl against the storm, and the mouth that wants to open and speak (or laugh) is choked by the cumbersome body of a huge, black snake; the weak creature of the nihilistic will, which strangles wild tigers in its heavy coils in the sultry atmosphere of the jungle, swathed in creeping mist and strange vegetation.

Given a pessimistic interpretation, the Eternal Return does nothing other than guide the snake into the open mouth in horrific recurrence of reactive forces – the Eternal Return of the Same in an endless cycle. But this is also an absurdity, since a nihilistic becoming could not be eternally affirmed (without degenerating into an epidemic of suicide or, worse, genocide from pity). To affirm the Eternal Return, the head of the snake has to be bitten off, its dry scales and cold blood spat out of the mouth – phasing the one who spits out into another becoming, another sensibility, when the urge to die has gone: becoming active, the thought of the Overman. The return is completed by the rule which turns negation into the negation of the reactive forces themselves. Nihilism no longer expresses itself as the protection of the weak, the junta mapping the *Kampfplatz* determining the space of evaluation and politics after their revolutionary victory, but their self-destruction. In this sense, we can see the Eternal Return as "the most extreme form of nihilism." [PF]

In this accomplished will to complete self-annihilation, it is not just that active forces become reactive, but that the reactive forces are themselves denied and obliterated in an immense, suicidal zero. This, in itself, is an active operation, an active destruction – the response of the strong who, testing their lives against the rule of the Eternal Return and finding them lacking, will their own decline in a dice throw which gambles on their future value – the Overman; the recurrence of this phase space of transvaluation: overcoming pushed further and further towards the alien distance.

5. "THE GENIUS OF THE HEART".

Perhaps the fate of all this insurgency is to be reprocessed through the digestive system of reactive force. What were once weapons, camouflage, survival tactics in a war of becoming, shedding being like a second skin, finally crystallize into axioms, concepts, truths – all so immortal, righteous, and *boring*. The madman who scampers into the marketplace, barking like a rabid dog about the death of God, may turn out to be a prophet. But he is also a fool – driven by his exploding neurophysiology to sacrifice himself in the here and now in favour of a future which may have already been digested by the system. Speculating on a future index, which attacks the securities of the present, language itself becomes a war machine, continually camouflaging itself to avoid capture – politely at war with itself, fighting poetry with prose and vice versa, gloating over its own inadequacy to translate itself, or anything else, into anything remotely comprehensible to anyone who is not similarly driven off the rails. But even then, mocking voices carried on evening sunbeams, streaming out of the paranoid heart of vestigial humanity, relentlessly pursue the madman through the twilight, repeating this: "You said poets lie too much. But what, in the end, are you? Only a fool! Only a poet! A liar and a traitor, unfit to speak in your own defence. A beast."

Embracing romantic decadence for a moment, the madman feels his isolation bite hard – with venomous fangs. Apparently alone on a beach, the survivor of a shipwreck, and waiting for a friend, he answers the sunbeams in the affirmative – pleading "guilty as charged," and taking up the refrain: "hundreds of thousands of experiments are made – changing the nourishment, the mode of living, and the environment of the body. Modes of consciousness and evaluation in the body, all kinds of pleasure and pain, are signs of these changes and experiments. In the end, it is not a question of man: man is to be overcome." [PF]

"If I could not derive strength from myself, if I had to totally rely on the world outside to encourage me, comfort me, make me happy – where would I be? What would I be? There really were moments, even whole periods, in my life when a single word of encouragement, or a friendly clutch at my hand would have been the best kind of medicine – and it was precisely then that I was abandoned by all those I thought I could rely on, and could have done me such kindnesses. I no longer expect this now: it's all so meaningless." [L]

Filtering these points through the moment, I begin to remember what I wanted in all those times of crisis. The sight of gleaming knives and forceps on the psychological operating table. Those times of crisis themselves. All those restless, bitter days; days of blinding sickness; all those loveless nightmares, for all time. Memory is fluid. Drifting through the Eternal Return, I slip into the madman's skin....

—Stephen Metcalf, November 1995

HAMMER
OF THE GODS

Apocalyptic Texts
For The Criminally Insane

FRIEDRICH NIETZSCHE

"You tremble, carcass? You would tremble even more
if you knew where I am going to take you!"
—*Vicomte de Turenne*

CHAPTER ONE

DEAD GOD

The Madman

Have you not heard the story of the madman who lit up a lantern in the radiant hours of morning, ran into the market place, and cried out: "I seek God! I seek God!" – Since many of the people who did not believe in God were gathered there, he provoked a great deal of laughter. Is he lost? asked one. Has he lost his way like a child? asked another. Is he hiding? Is he afraid of us? Has he departed on a long voyage? Or has he emigrated? – Thus they howled and laughed.

The madman leapt into their midst, piercing them with his stare. "Where has God gone?" he cried out; "I will tell you: we have killed him – you and I have killed him. We are all his murderers. But how could we have done this? How did we manage to drink away the ocean? Who gave us the sponge with which we wiped away the horizon? To where is it moving now? To where are we going? Running away from all suns? Are we not continually plunging down? Backwards, sidewards, forwards, in all directions? Does any up or down remain? Are

---

we not drifting as through an infinite nothing? Who does not yet feel the icy breath of empty space? Is it not becoming ever colder? Do we not need to light fires in the morning? Do we still not hear the sound of the gravediggers who are busy burying God? Do we still not smell anything of divine putrefaction? Gods also decompose. God is dead. God will always stay dead. And we have killed him.

"How can we console ourselves, we, the murderers of all murderers? What was once holiest and mightiest of all in the universe has bled to death under our knives: who will wipe away his blood? With what kind of water may we clean ourselves? What festivals of atonement, what sacred games shall we have to invent? Is the enormity of this murder too great for us? Must we not ourselves become gods merely to seem worthy of it? There has never been a greater deed; and those who are born after us, for the sake of this deed, will belong to a higher history than all history up until this moment."

With that, the madman became silent and contemplated his listeners again; and they, too, fell silent and stared at him in shock. At last, he hurled his lantern to the ground, smashed it into pieces, and walked away. Then he said: "I have come too early. My time has not yet come. This monumental event is still to come, it still wanders; it has yet to reach the ears of men. Thunder and lightning need time to strike; the light from the stars needs time to reach the earth; deeds, though long since done, still need time to be seen and heard. This deed is still even further from them in the distance than the most distant stars – *and yet they have done it themselves.*"

It was told further that, later that day, the madman forced his way into several churches and struck up his *requiem aeternum deo*. Dragged out and forced to account for himself, he is always said to have offered nothing more in reply than: "What in the end are all these churches if they are not the graves and sepulchres of God?" [GS]

O, my brothers, when I told you to destroy the good and shatter the law tablets of the good, only then did I set humanity sailing upon its furthest oceans.

It is now that the great horror, the great prospect, the great affliction, the great loathing, the great sea-sickness arrive.

The good taught you to believe in false shores and false security; you were born into and held captive in the lies of the good. Everything has been twisted and warped down to its core by the good.

But he who first landed upon the territory of 'Man' also discovered the oceans of 'Human Future'. Now you shall all be sailors – brave, patient voyagers!

The sea is stormy. Everything is at sea.

What of fatherlands! Our helm points out into the distance, it wants to sail *away*; far, far away; out to where the land of our children lies! [Z]

After Buddha was dead, his shadow was still shown to be lingering for centuries in a cave – a colossal, grotesque shadow. God is dead; but, knowing the ways of men, there may still exist caves in which his shadow will be exhibited for thousands of years. And we still have to eradicate his shadow too. [GS]

If the idea of god is eradicated, so too must also be the feeling of sin as a transgression against divine precepts, as a contamination of a creature otherwise consecrated to God. What remains after this has gone is probably very closely entwined in and related to the fear of punishment by a secular justice, or fear of men's disdain; but discontent caused by a pang of conscience, the sharpest sting of all in the experience of guilt, is aborted at its source when one realizes that, regardless of whether or not one's actions may have transgressed human tradition, human laws, human regulations, one has still not jeopardized the "eternal salvation of the soul" and its relation to the divinity. When man finally succeeds in convincing himself intellectually that all actions are unconditionally necessary and utterly irresponsible, and he embeds this conviction in his flesh and blood, then all vestiges of the pang of conscience vanish too. [HH]

When in love with a woman, we easily begin to nurture a kind of hatred resulting from all of the repulsive natural functions to which any woman is subject. We would rather not think of all this, but in a moment when our soul touches upon these matters, it shrugs and regards nature with scorn. We feel affronted; nature appears to defile our possessions with the filthiest of hands. At this point, we refuse to pay any attention to physiology and secretly decree: "I will hear no more about the fact that a human being is something more than soul and form." For all lovers "the human being beneath the skin" is an unspeakable horror, a blasphemy against God and love.

Just as lovers feel about nature and natural functions, so every worshipper of God and his "holy omnipotence" felt in the past: all that has been said about nature by astronomers, geologists, physiologists, or physicians, he took to be a defilement of his most prized possessions and, as such, an attack – and a very shameless attack at that. Even the term "natural law" to him had all the resonance of an assault against God; and he would really have preferred to see all of mechanics derived from acts of a moral or arbitrary will. But since nobody was able to perform this service for him, he *ignored* nature and mechanics as far as he was able and lived in a dream. O, how these men of the past knew how to dream without even finding it necessary to fall asleep! And how we modern men still master this art all too well! It is sufficient to love, to hate, to desire, to merely feel – and straight away the spirit and power of the dream overcome us, and, coldly scornful of all hazards, we scale the most dangerous paths to reach the roofs and spires of fantasy – without any sense of vertigo, as if we were born to climb, we modern sleepwalkers! We artists! We ignore what is natural. We are starstruck and besotted with God. We roam, motionless as death, yet still awake, on heights that we do not see as heights, but as plains – as our safety. [GS]

When water has boards thrown over it so that it may be walked upon, when gangways and railings stretch across the river: he who says "Everything is in flux," is not believed by anyone.

Even idiots contradict him. "What was that?" say the idiots, "everything is in flux? But boards and railings lie *over* the stream!

"*Over* the stream everything is fixed in place, all the values of things, the bridges, the concepts, all good and evil: all are *fixed in place!*"

But when the hard winter arrives, the tamer of bestial streams, then even the cleverest among men learn mistrust. From then on, it is no longer only the idiots who say: "Is it not true that everything is meant to stand still?"

"Fundamentally, everything stands still" – this is a true doctrine for the winter, made for infertile seasons, made for hibernators.

"Fundamentally, everything stands still" – but the thawing wind demonstrates the reverse.

The thawing wind is an ox, and not an ox that ploughs fields, to be sure – it is a raging ox, a destroyer that breaks ice with its furious horns. And even ice, itself, *breaks gangways!*

Is it not true, my brothers, that everything is now in flux? Do you not see how all railings and gangways have fallen into the water, and have amounted to nothing? Who is still able to grasp after 'good' and 'evil'?

"Woe to us! And hail to us! The thawing wind blows!" – Cry this out on every street, O my brothers! [Z]

The Four Errors
Man has been educated by his errors. Firstly, he never saw himself completely; secondly, he bestowed fictitious attributes upon himself; thirdly, he placed himself uppermost in a false scale of rank in relation to animals and nature; fourthly, he invented and reinvented new tables of goods and always presumed them, at least for a time, to be eternal and unconditional: as a result of these, one and then another human drive and state held first place and was venerated because it was regarded so highly. If we were to eradicate the effects of these four errors, we would also eradicate humanity, humaneness, and 'human dignity'. [GS]

Life No Argument
We have mapped out for ourselves a world in which we can bear to live – by positing bodies, lines, planes, causes and effects, motion and rest, form and content. Without these articles of faith nobody could tolerate life – but that is no proof of the truth of any of them. Life is no argument. The conditions of life may include error. [GS]

On The Origin Of Our Evaluations

We can position our body in space. From this we gain exactly the same image of it as we have of the solar system, and the distinction between all that is organic and all that is non-organic is no longer obvious. Hitherto, the movements of the stars were conceptualized as effects produced by beings conscious of a purpose. We no longer have any use for this explanation, and, as far as bodily motion and change is concerned, it has been a long time since we abandoned belief in explanation in terms of a consciousness that determines purposes. The great majority of movements have nothing at all to do with consciousness or sensation. Sensation and thought are both extremely unimportant and rare in relation to the innumerable events that take place at every moment.

On the other hand, we notice that a purposiveness governs the smallest events – a purposiveness that is beyond our understanding: planning, selection, organization, reparation, and so-on. We come upon an activity that previously would have been ascribed to a higher and more comprehensive intellect than that which we know. We learn to think less highly of all that is conscious; we learn to forget responsibility for ourselves – since the conscious, purposive products we are thought in terms of form such an insignificant part of us. We sense almost nothing of the multiplicity of influences which operate upon us at every moment – e.g. air, electricity. There could be many forces at work that we never sense but which continually influence us. Pleasure and pain are very rare and scarce manifestations compared with the innumerable stimuli that cells and organs exert on one another all the time.

We are entering the phase in which consciousness becomes modest. We understand the conscious ego itself only as a tool put to the service of a higher, comprehensive intellect; and then find ourselves able to ask if it is not the case that all conscious acts of will, all conscious purposes, all evaluations are no more than the means by which something completely different from what becomes present to consciousness is to be achieved. We may think that it is a question of our pleasure and displeasure. But pleasure and displeasure could be means through which we have to achieve something outside our consciousness. It needs to be demonstrated to what extent all that is conscious lies on the surface, how an action and the image of an action diverge, how little we know of what precedes an action, how stupid are our feelings of "free will" or "cause and effect", how thoughts, images, and words are only signs of thought as such; the inexplicable nature of all action; the superficial idiocy of all veneration and blame; how essential are fictions and conceit to all in which we consciously live; how all our words signify fictions (and also our affects); and, finally, how all the threads binding men to each other depend on the transmission and conjunction of these fictions, while, in a fundamental sense, the real bond (through procreation) drifts off in its unknown way. Does belief in all these fictitious ideals really alter men? Or is it that the whole realm of ideas and evaluations is only a secondary articulation of an unknown process of change? *Do these really exist:* will, purposes, thoughts, values? Is conscious life, in its entirety, no more than a reflected image? Even if we could be shown to be correct in assuming evaluation to determine the nature of humanity, at base something quite different is going on! If we suppose that purposiveness in nature could be judged without first assuming the existence of an ego that posits purposes – could it still be the case that *our* positing of purposes, our willing, etc., is only a sign language for something completely different: i.e. something that does not will – something unconscious? The most fleeting reflection of natural expediency in the organic, and no different from it?

Perhaps the whole evolution of the spirit is just a question of the body. It is the process of development of a higher body looming in our sensibility. The organic is rising to different and higher levels. Our thirst for knowledge of nature is a means through which the body strives to perfect itself. [PF]

All of Descarte's arguments end, where they begin, in this: "there is thinking: therefore there is something that thinks." This means postulating as "true *a priori*" our belief in the concept of substance – the belief that where there is thought there must be something that thinks is a repetition of the custom of grammar which always adds a doer to the deed. But this is not the substantiation of a fact: it is a postulate of logic and metaphysics. Following the co-ordinates mapped by Descartes one does not reach the truth of a realm of absolute certainty – but only the fact of a very strong belief.

In producing the proposition "there is thinking therefore there are thoughts", one simply produces a tautology. All that is in question – the "reality" of thought – is never reached. In this form, the "apparent reality" of thought cannot be denied. But what Descartes wanted was that thought should have not an *apparent* reality, but reality *in itself*. [PF]

We have learned better. We have become more modest in all respects. We no longer trace the origin of man back to the "spirit" or to the "divinity." We have ranked him back among the animals. We believe him to be the strongest of the animals on account of his supreme cunning. His spirituality issues from this. On the other hand, we must beware of the kind of vanity which strives to express itself here: the vanity which believes man to be the great secret purpose of animal evolution. Man is categorically *not* the crown of all creation: every creature stands at his side, at the same stage of perfection. And, even here, we assert too much. Man is, in a certain sense, the most unsuccessful animal, the most sick, the animal which has most dangerously deviated from its instincts – but, by that token, also the most *interesting!*

With regard to the animals, Descartes was the first thinker who, with considerable courage, dared to think of animals as machines: the whole of the science of physiology is given over to proving this assertion. Logically, we do not exclude man from this, as Descartes did: our current knowledge of man is actual knowledge to the extent that it is knowledge of him as a machine. Hitherto, man was endowed with "free will" as a gift from a higher order. Today, we have taken this will away from him – in the sense that will can no longer be taken to be an intellectual faculty. What was formerly known as "will" only designates a product; a kind of individual reaction which necessarily crystallizes on a host of partly contradictory, partly consonant stimuli – the will no longer "effects" nor "moves" anything. Formerly one could see in man's consciousness, in his "spirit", the justification for his higher origin, his divine nature. To attain perfection man was told to suck his senses back into himself like the withdrawing head of a tortoise, to renounce any kind of commerce with all that is terrestrial, to forget his mortal body: then the larger portion of him would survive as "pure spirit". We have learned better in this case, too: becoming conscious, or "spirit", is a symptom of imperfection in the organism, an experimenting, a fumbling, a botching, and a kind of labour through which an unnecessarily large measure of nervous energy is expended. We refute the idea that anything can be made perfect as long as it continues to be made conscious. "Pure spirit" is just a pure idiocy. If we remove the nervous system and the senses, the mortal body, we miscalculate – and nothing more than that! [A]

The concept of substance issues from the concept of the subject, not the reverse. If we eliminate the soul, the subject as such, the foundation for substance in general vanishes. One processes intensities of being, one is stripped of all that which *has* being.

The subject is the term with which we designate our belief in a unity which underlies all the manifold impulses of the highest feeling of reality. We take this belief to be the *effect* of a single cause – we believe so immovably in our belief that we come to conceptualize "truth", "reality", and "substance" for its sake. "The subject" is the fiction we supply ourselves with that says that many similar states in us are the effect of a single substratum. But it is we who, in the first place, create the "similarity" of these states – our adjusting them and making them similar is the fact, not their inherent similarity – (this latter point needs to be denied). [PF]

Must the whole of philosophy not, in the end, reveal the preconditions upon which the whole process rests? – Our belief in the "ego" as a substance, as the only reality from which we can possibly ascribe reality to exterior things? The oldest form of "realism" is finally illuminated – the whole of the religious history of mankind is revealed to be the history of the superstition of the soul. And here we reach a limit: all of our thought involves this belief (with all its concepts of substance, accident, deed, doer, etc.) To let go of it means this: to no longer be able to think.

A belief, no matter how indispensable it might be for the preservation of a species, has nothing to do with truth. For example, the fact is that we need to believe in time, space, and motion – but we do not feel compelled to ascribe an absolute reality to them. [PF]

All that enters our consciousness as a "unity" is always incredibly complex. We only ever possess an appearance of unity. The phenomenon of the body is a richer, more obvious, more palpable phenomenon – to be discussed, first, in terms of methodology, without reaching any decision as to its final significance. [PF]

My Hypotheses
The subject as multiplicity. Pain as intellectual and totally dependent on the judgement "harmful" projected outwards. Pleasure is a kind of pain. The effect is always "unconscious". The inferred and imagined cause is transposed onto what follows in time. The only force that exists produces the same effect as the will: it commands other subjects, which change as a result. The continuous, fleeting, transitory nature of the subject. "Mortal soul". Number as a form of perspective. [PF]

Why start with the body and physiology? – Because here we attain the correct idea of the exact nature of our subject-unity: namely, as the governor at the head of a communal body (not as a "soul" or "life force"), and also how these governors depend upon all that they rule, and how an order of rank and division of labour are the conditions making possible the whole and its parts. In the same way, we investigate how living unities continually emerge and die out, and why the subject is not eternal; why the struggle manifests in commanding and obeying; and why a fluctuating index of the limits of power is part of life. The relative ignorance in which the governor is kept as regards individual activities, and even disturbances, within the common body is one of the conditions upon which the exercise of rule depends. Thus we are also able to evaluate *not knowing*, the ability to see things on a larger scale; simplification, falsification, perspectivism. The important thing is that we understand that the ruler and his subjects are of the same type – all feeling, willing, thinking – and that wherever we notice movement in a body, we learn to realize that there is a subjective, invisible life adhering to it. Movement is symbolism for the eye – it communicates that something has been felt, willed, or thought. [PF]

Consciousness
Consciousness is merely the last and most recent development of the organic, and, as such, is also all that is most incomplete and precarious. Consciousness gives rise to a multitude of errors that lead to the premature death of an animal or a man – a death which "exceeds destiny", as Homer put it. If the preservative conjunction of the instincts was less powerful, and if it did not function, in general, as a regulating mechanism, then humanity would necessarily die, as a result of its misjudgements and fantasies, with its eyes wide open; as a result of its lack of rigour and its gullibility – in short, as a result of its consciousness. Without the former, humanity would have ceased to exist a long time ago.

Before a function has fully developed and matured, it poses a threat to the organism; and it is just as well if, in the interim, it is subjected to some kind of tyranny. Consciousness is tyrannized – not least by our belief in it. One takes it to be the core of man; all that is continuous, eternal, final, and original in him. One takes consciousness to be a formative magnitude. One denies that it grows, that it is irregular. One believes it to constitute the "unity of the organism".

This absurd overinvestment and misunderstanding of consciousness has functional consequences in that it hinders consciousness from developing too quickly. Since they believe that they possess consciousness, men have not strained themselves too much in its acquisition; and things have never altered much in this respect. The task of ingesting knowledge and making it instinctive is only now beginning to dawn on humanity, and is still not clearly visible to the naked eye. It is a task that has only been noticed by those who have understood that hitherto we have lived by our errors alone, and that all our consciousness relates to errors. [GS]

On The Aim Of Science
What? Science should aim to give men as much pleasure and as little displeasure as possible? What would it mean if pleasure and displeasure were so tightly connected that whoever wanted as much as possible of the one must also suffer as much as possible of the other? – That whoever wanted to learn how to savour "jubilation up to the heavens" would also have to suffer "depression to the point of death"? Because things may well be like this. The Stoics certainly believed things to be ordered in this way and, to their credit, they were consistent in that they wanted as little pleasure as possible in order for them to suffer as little displeasure as possible in their lives.

Right now you have this choice: either *as little displeasure as possible*, numbness in brief – and, in the final analysis, all socialists and other politicians have no right to promise any more than this – or as much displeasure as possible, as the price to be paid for an abundance of subtle, unknown pleasures. If you decide in favour of the former, and desire to cut away at the thresholds of human pain, you will also have to reduce the level of the capacity for joy. Science is capable of serving either end. At the moment it is better known for its power to deprive man of his joys and make him colder, like a statue, a stoic. But it could also be found to be the great conductor of pain. At this point, the possibility of its counterforce opens up: it makes immense new galaxies of joy explode. [GS]

What is the most intense pleasure enjoyed by men who live in the state of war characterizing those small, continually threatened communities governed by the strictest mores? In other words, what is this for vigourous, vengeful, vicious, untrusting souls who prepare themselves to face all that is most terrible, and are hardened by the deprivations required by mores? It is the enjoyment of cruelty. In circumstances such as these, it will be listed among the virtues of such a soul if it is inventive and insatiable in its lust for cruelty. The community feels nourished by cruelty, and finds itself temporarily able to shake itself out of the gloom of perpetual anxiety and caution. Cruelty belongs among the archaic forms of humanity's festive joys. One might suppose that the gods also feel nourished and festive when offered the spectacle of cruelty – and it is thus that the idea insinuates its way into the world that voluntary suffering, torture that one inflicts upon oneself, has value.

Gradually, a cultural milieu takes shape around this idea: all luxurious shows of well-being begin to arouse suspicion, and all severe and painful states begin to be viewed with confidence.

The concept of the "most virtuous" member of the community comes to embody the moral value of frequent suffering, deprivation, a severe way of life, and self-mortification – not as a means to the end of self-control and the desire for individual happiness, but as a virtue that makes the community appear good in the eyes of the evil gods, which reaches them in plumes of smoke from some endless atonement on a sacrificial altar. All the spiritual leaders who were successful in moving something in the inert but fertile muck of their mores needed both madness and voluntary torture to secure faith – and, first of all and most importantly, their faith in themselves. The more their own spirit moved along untried paths and was tortured by conscience and fear, the more cruelly they violated their own flesh, desires, and health – as if they wanted to offer their gods a substitute satisfaction, just in case they were enraged at the sight of customs that had been neglected and stirred themselves to fight against these new causes.

Let us beware of believing that we have completely distanced ourselves from such a logic of feeling. Let only the bravest souls probe their own feelings about this. Every single step on the field of free thought and organic life has been fought for by means of spiritual and physical torments. Not just moving forwards but all moving, motion, and change have immolated countless martyrs – throughout the pathfinding millennia about which people think nothing when they speak, as is their habit, about "world history": that pathetically small segment of human existence. And even according to this so-called world history, which is only ever a basic furore over the latest news, there is really no issue bigger than the primordial tragedy of the martyrs who wanted to move the swamps.

Nothing has been more costly than this tiny fragment of human reason and the feeling of freedom which constitutes our pride. It is precisely this pride which makes it almost impossible for us to reckon with the incredible timespan characterized by the mores which antedate "world history" as the real and decisive history in the formation of the nature of humanity – times when suffering was a virtue, revenge was a virtue, the violation of reason was a virtue; while well-being was a danger, madness was divine, and change was immoral and pregnant with disaster.

If you think that all this has changed, and that humanity has changed its nature, well then! – you who think you know men ought to better acquaint yourselves with yourselves! [D]

The idea of God twists all that is straight and makes all that stands up dizzy. What is this? Would time be abolished and all that is transitory no more than a lie?

To think like this makes the human frame totter in dizziness and vertigo, and brings waves of nausea to the stomach: I call it the dizzy affliction to think such a thing.

I call it evil and misanthropic to think like this – all these teachings about the one and the perfect and the immovable and the sufficient and the intransitory.

All that is intransitory – *that* is but an image! And all the poets lie too much.

All the best images and parables should speak both of time and becoming: they should be a eulogy for and a justification of all that is transitory.

Truly, I have followed paths through a hundred souls, through a hundred cradles, through a hundred birth agonies. I have taken my leave of many things, I know the heart-breaking pains of the last hours before departure.

But my creative will, my destiny, would have it be so.

This will drew me away from God and all gods. What could there be to create if gods – existed?

Time and time again, this ardent, creative will drives me to mankind; thus it brings the hammer down upon the stone.

Sleeping in the stone I see an image, the image of all my visions!

My hammer crashes fiercely against its prison. [Z]

Congenital Defect Of All Philosophers
All philosophers are afflicted with the same defect – they start with modern man and presume they can arrive at their goal by analyzing him. They instinctively allow man to hang in the air

before them as an *aeterna veritas* (eternal truth), something which remains constant despite all turmoil, a constant measure of things. But everything that philosophers assert about the nature of man is really no more than an assertion about man confined to a very limited time span. Thus the congenital defect of all philosophers is a profound lack of historical sense. Some have even gone so far as to take the most recent form of man, as it developed under the imprint of certain forms of religion or political events, as the evolved, fixed form from which one must proceed.

The philosopher sees 'instincts' in modern man and presumes that they belong to the permanent facts of human nature, and that they can, insofar as this is accepted, provide the key to the understanding of the world in general. The whole of this teleology turns upon the ability to speak of the man of the last four thousand years as if he were eternal, the direction towards which all things have been rushing since the beginning. However, everything has evolved; there are no *eternal facts*, no absolute truths. Henceforth, *historical philosophizing* is necessary, along with the virtue of modesty. [HH]

Resonance
All intense states carry with them a certain resonance of related feelings and states; they seem to agitate memory. Something within us remembers becoming conscious of similar states and their origins. Habitual and rapid associations between thoughts and feelings are configured which, following upon one another with lightning speed, are eventually experienced not as complexes but as *unities*. It is in this sense that one conceives of moral feelings, religious feelings, as if they all formed unities, when in truth they are rivers with a hundred sources and tributaries. It is often the case that the unity of the word does not attest to the unity of the thing. [HH]

The Error Of The Imaginary Cause

To start from a dream: onto a given sensation, e.g. the result of a gunshot somewhere in the distance is transposed onto a cause – often a whole novella, in which the dreamer is the main protagonist. The sensation persists as a kind of resonance: it lingers until the cause-creating drive allows it to burst into the foreground – no longer as a chance occurrence, but as "meaning". The gunshot finds its way in in a causal way, in an apparent inversion of time. That which comes afterwards, the force of motivation, is experienced first; often connected to a hundred details which flash by like lightning, and the shot follows. What happened? The ideas produced by a certain condition have been taken to be the cause of that condition. We continue to act in the same way while awake. The majority of our feelings – every kind of restraint, pressure, stress, or outburst in the interconnection of our organs, excite our cause-creating drive. We want to find a reason for feeling as we do – for the feeling of well-being, or of illness. It is never enough for us to simply establish the fact that we feel what we feel. We only acknowledge this fact, we only become conscious of it, when we have connected it to a motivating cause of some kind. The memory, which becomes active in a case like this without our being aware of it, recalls earlier, similar states and the causal connections which have grown out of them – but not how they have grown out of causality. The belief that these ideas, the secondary processes of consciousness, are causes is also suggested by the memory. Thus a habit forms around a certain causal interpretation which actually prevents, and even rules out, an investigation of the cause. [TI]

Among Germans it will be understood at once when I say that philosophy has been contaminated by theology. The Protestant pastor is the godfather of German philosophy – Protestantism itself is its original sin. My definition of Protestantism: the half-hearted paralysis of Christianity and of reason. If things were otherwise, then why was so much rejoicing heard among German academics – three quarters of whom were the sons of pastors and teachers – at the appearance of Kant? For what was the German conviction, which still has its echoes, that with Kant things were taking a turn for the better? Once again, all the theological drives in the German scholar legislated all that was possible. A secret route to the old ideal was revealed – the concept of the "real world", the concept of morality as the *essence* of the world – (these are the two most vicious errors in existence) – were, thanks to the exercise of a crafty, slippery kind of scepticism, rendered, if not demonstrable, then certainly no longer refutable.

But reason, the *right of reason*, does not extend as far as this. One makes of reality an "appearance", bringing a completely fabricated world of "being" into reality. Kant's success is the success of a theologian. German integrity was far from firm and Kant, like Luther and Leibniz before him, was merely one more constraint upon its development. [A]

A few words against Kant as a moralist. Any virtue should be our invention, the most personal form of our defence, and necessary to this end. In any other sense, it is dangerous. Anything that does not condition our life *damages* it: virtue believed in merely out of respect for the concept of "virtue", as Kant would have it, is dangerous. "Virtue", "duty", "good in itself", depersonalized and universalized, are ghosts, expressions of decline – the ultimate exhaustion of life, the despotism of Königsberg. All the profound laws of preservation and growth entail the reverse of this: they demand that each of us should devise their own virtue, their own categorical imperative. A people which mistakes its duty for the concept of duty in general will die out. Nothing leads to a more complete ruin than "impersonal" duty, that sacrifice to the

Moloch of abstraction. Kant's categorical imperative should have been recognized to be mortally dangerous! But the theological instinct offered it protection.

An action which is impelled by the instinct for life has, in the joy of performing that action, proof that it is the right action. But any nihilist with a gut full of Christian dogma takes joy to be an objection. What could destroy more quickly than to labour, to think, to feel, without a deep-seated inner necessity for this to be the case; to do it without a profound personal choice and joylessly? This would be a virtual recipe for *decadence* – and even for idiocy. After all, Kant himself became a senile idiot. And this deadly spider continues to count as the ultimate German philosopher.... Did Kant not see in the French Revolution the transition from the non-organic to the organic form of the state? Did he not ask himself if there was an event which could only be explained by means of a moral predisposition on the part of humanity with which the "tendency of man to seek the good" could be proved once and for all? Kant's answer was this: "It's the Revolution!" The instinct to miscalculate in every respect, anti-nature as driving force, German decadence as philosophy – that is what Kant means to me! [A]

From A Doctoral Exam
"What is the purpose of higher education?" – To turn man into a machine. – "By what means is this to be achieved?" – He must learn to feel bored. – "How is this to be achieved?" – By means of the concept of duty. – "Who is the model for this?" – The philologist; he teaches mindless toil. – "Who is the ultimate man?" – The civil servant. – "Which philosophy provides the best model for the civil servant?" – Kant's: the civil servant as thing in itself set above the civil servant as appearance as judge. [TI]

Number

Our laws of number were inscribed on the basis of the originally prevailing error that a series of identical things exist (whereas, in fact, nothing is identical) or, at very least, that there are things (but there is no "thing".) The presumption of multiplicity always assumes that there is *something*; something which occurs repeatedly: and it is precisely here that error rules – we invent entities, unities, which simply do not exist.

Whenever we establish the truth of something scientifically, we are always already calculating in terms of certain false quantities; but since these quantities are at least *constant* (for example, our experience of time and space), the findings of science acquire an unqualified rigour and certainty in their relationship to one another. When Kant writes that "Reason does not invent its laws from nature, but dictates them to her," this is true only with respect to the *concept of nature* we are compelled to delimit her in terms of (Nature = world as idea, as error), that is, the summation of a series of errors of reason.

In a world that is *not* our idea, the laws of number no longer apply: they are valid only in the human world. [HH]

I have learned to separate that which is the cause of acting from that which is the cause of acting in a particular way, in a particular direction, towards a particular goal. The first type of cause is a quantum of dammed-up energy that waits to be used up in some way, for some purpose; whereas the second type is something insignificant when compared with this energy, and, for the most part, little more than an accident towards which this quantum of energy expends itself in a particular way – a match touching against a ton of gunpowder. I include among these little accidents and 'matches' all so-called 'purposes' and, to an even greater degree, so-called 'vocations': they are all relatively aleatory, arbitrary, and almost indifferent in relation to the immense quantum of energy which presses to be expended in some way. The received view is different: people are used to considering goals, purposes, vocations, etc., to be the *driving force*, in accordance with a very ancient error; but it is nothing more than the *directing force* – the helmsman has been mistaken for the engine: and often, not even the helmsman but the directing force.

Is the 'goal', the 'purpose', often any more than an embellishing pretext, a vain self-deception that comes after an event, that refuses to acknowledge that the ship *follows* the current into which it accidentally strays? – that it 'wills' to travel in that direction because *it has to?* – that it has a direction, of this we can be sure, but no helmsman whatsoever? [GS]

If one renounces Christian belief, one also denies oneself the right to Christian morality. Christianity is a system; a consistent, rigorous, and complete view of things. If one removes from it a fundamental idea, the belief in God, one smashes the whole thing to pieces – and one no longer holds anything of any consequence in one's hands. Christianity presupposes that man does not know, and cannot know, what is good and what is evil for himself: he believes in God, who is alone in knowing this. Christian morality is an imperative: it has a transcendental origin; it is therefore beyond all criticism, or any right to criticize; it is true only if the idea of God is true – it stands or falls with the belief in God. [TI]

The Myth Of Intelligible Freedom

The entire history of the feelings by means of which we hold a person to be responsible, so-called moral feelings, is divided into the following phases. First, we designate particular acts good or evil without considering their motives, on the basis of their consequences – whether beneficial or harmful. But we soon forget the origin of these words and imagine the quality "good" or "evil" to be inherent to the acts in themselves. We no longer consider their consequences. This is the same mistake that is made by language when it calls the stone itself hard, the tree itself green – we take effects to be causes. After this, we assign good or evil to the motives behind these acts, and regard the acts themselves to be morally neutral. Then we go even further and cease to invest a particular motive with good or evil, and find it in the entire nature of a man – the motive emerges from him in the same way that a plant emerges from the soil. We make man responsible in turn for the effects of his actions, then for the effects of his actions, then for his actions themselves, then for the motives informing his actions, and, finally, for his nature. In the end, we find that his nature cannot be responsible for anything – since it, itself, is an inevitable consequence and outgrowth of the forms and influences of past and present; which means that man cannot be made responsible for anything – neither for his nature, nor his motives, nor his actions, nor the effects of his actions. Thus we come to realize that the history of moral feelings is the history of an error. This error is called "responsibility", and it turns upon the axis of another error – that of "freedom of the will".

On the other hand, Schopenhauer came to the following conclusions: if certain actions lead to displeasure (a "feeling of guilt"), then a responsibility must exist: because their would be no reason for this displeasure if not only all human actions took place out of necessity (which, according to my insight, is what they do), but also if man acquired his whole nature out of these same necessities (which Schopenhauer denies). From the fact of man's displeasure, Schopenhauer assumes that he has proved that man somehow must have had a freedom, a freedom which did not just determine his actions, but his whole nature: freedom, that is, to be this way or that way; to choose not to act this way or the other. According to

Schopenhauer, "operari" (doing), the realm of strict causality, necessity, and lack of responsibility, follows on from "esse" (being), the realm of freedom and responsibility. The feeling of displeasure seems to be part of "operari" (it is mistaken in this), but, in truth, it is a function of "esse" – which is the exercise of a free will, the first cause of an individual's existence. Man becomes what he *wants* to be; his purpose precedes his existence.

But here we conclude falsely if we think that we can derive the justification, the rational legitimacy, of this displeasure, from the fact that it exists. From this mistaken calculation, Schopenhauer arrives at his stupendous conclusion of "intelligible freedom". But the feeling of displeasure after the deed is done need not be at all rational. In fact, it is completely irrational, because it rests on the mistaken assumption that the deed did not necessarily have to take place. Because he thinks that he is free (but not because he *is* free), man feels guilt and the pangs of the bad conscience.

This feeling of displeasure is a habit that can be given up. There are men who do not feel it at all, even after doing the same things that make others feel it. Connected to the growth of custom and culture, it is not a constant thing, and, perhaps, only appears within a fairly short period of world history. [HH]

No-one is accountable in the slightest for his existence, or for being constituted as he is, or for being found among the conditions and in the surroundings he lives in. The fatality of his nature cannot be disentangled from the fatality of all that which has gone before and all that which will be. He is *not* the result of some special design, a will, or a purpose; he is *not* the subject of some attempt to reach up to an "ideal of man", an "ideal of happiness", or an "ideal of morality" – it is ridiculous to seek to deliver his nature to some kind of purpose. We invented the concept of 'purpose': in reality, there is no purpose.... One is necessary, a portion of fate, one belongs to the whole, one *is* the whole – and nothing exists against which one could judge, measure, compare, condemn our being – that would be to judge, measure, compare, and condemn the whole.... Nothing exists apart from the whole.... We deny God. In denying God, we deny accountability – and it is only in this that redemption lies. [TI]

We never accuse nature of immorality when it sends us a thunderstorm and soaks us: so why bother calling the harmful man immoral? It is because, in the first case, we assume necessity, and, in the second, the voluntary government of free will. But this is a mistaken distinction. Even intentional injury is not considered to be immoral in all circumstances: we will not hesitate to kill a gnat, simply because its buzzing annoys us; and we *intentionally* harm criminals to protect ourselves and society. In the first instance, the individual does harm intentionally for self-preservation, or to avoid irritation; in the second, the state does the harm. All kinds of morality allow the intentional inflicting of injury for the purpose of self-defence; that is, when it is a matter of self-preservation. But these two points are all that is required to explain all "evil" acts which men perpetrate against one another; one seeks to obtain pleasure and avoid displeasure – in some sense, it is always a matter of self-preservation. Socrates and Plato are right: in whatever he does, man always acts for the good; i.e. in a way that seems good (which is to say, useful) according to the level of his intelligence, the prevailing measure of his rationality. [HH]

If one has even the most residual superstition left in one's system, one can hardly entirely reject the idea that one is merely an embodiment, merely a mouthpiece, merely a medium for overpowering forces. The concept of revelation – in the sense that something, with indescribable certainty and subtlety, suddenly becomes obvious, visible, audible, something that rocks one down to the depths and throws one to the floor – that merely describes the facts. One hears, one no longer seeks; one accepts, one no longer asks who gives; a thought explodes like lightning, with necessity, without any hesitation with reference to its form. I never had any choice. [EH]

Everything happens involuntarily in the highest degree – but as in a storm of the feeling of freedom, of absolute power, of divinity. The involuntary nature of image and metaphor is the strangest case of all: one lacks any notion of what any metaphor or image *is* – everything unveils itself as the closest, most obvious, simplest expression. [EH]

But it is the *body* that is inspired: let us keep "the soul" out of it. [EH]

Let us beware of believing the world to be a living being. To where would it expand? On what would it feed? How would it grow and multiply? We possess some kind of notion of the nature of the organic; and it would be a mistake to interpret the extremely derivative, late, rare, accidental things that we perceive on the crust of the earth as something essential, universal, and eternal – as do the people who think of the universe as an organism. This makes me sick. Let us even beware of thinking of the universe as a machine: it is not constructed for a single purpose, and referring to it as a "machine" honours it far too greatly.

Let us beware of postulating everywhere anything as dignified as the cyclic motions of neighbouring stars; a momentary glance into the Milky Way incurs severe doubts as to whether or not there are far more uneven and contradictory movements there, as well as stars traversing eternally linear courses. The cosmic order we live in is an exception: this order, and the relative continuity that depends on this order have made possible an exception of exceptions – the formation of the organic. But the total character of the world is, in all eternity, chaos – not in the sense of a lack of necessity, but in the sense of a lack of order, of arrangement, form, beauty, wisdom, and all the other names we have for our aesthetic anthropomorphisms. Judged from the point of view of reason, failed attempts are by all standards the rule, exceptions are not the secret aim, and the entire musical box repeats its tune eternally, a tune which it would not be possible to call a melody – and, in the end, even the phrase "failed attempt" is too anthropomorphic and reproachful to apply. How could we reproach or even praise the universe? Let us beware of ascribing to it cruelty and unreason or their opposites: it is neither flawless, nor beautiful, nor noble; it could not even wish to become any of these things, it does not by any standard struggle to emulate man. None of our aesthetic or moral judgements apply to it. It has no instinct for self-preservation, nor any other instinct whatsoever, and it does not obey any laws. Let us beware of believing that there are laws in nature. All things that exist are necessities: there is no-one in command, no-one who obeys, no-one who transgresses. Once you realize that there is no purpose to all this, you also realize that there are no accidents; since the word "accident" only has meaning if measured against a world of purposes. Let us beware of conceiving of death as opposed to life. What lives is no more than a very rare type of what is already dead.

Let us beware of believing that the world always creates new things. There are no eternal, permanent substances. When will we ever divest ourselves of our caution and care? When will all these shadows of God finally stop darkening our minds? When will we finally accomplish a thoroughgoing *atheology of nature?* [GS]

It may be worth contemplating that the decisive event for the type of "free spirit" likely to ripen to perfection one day is a great separation, and that, before this moment, he is all the more a bound spirit, shackled forever in his corner, chained to his post. What binds most tightly? Which ties are almost too strong to be broken? Obligations, the awe pertaining to the young before all that is honoured by tradition, their gratitude to the earth out of which they grew, for the hand that beckoned to them to follow, for the altars at which they were taught to worship. For such people the great separation comes suddenly, like the shockwaves of an earthquake, devastating the young soul, tearing it apart, tearing it loose – it does not know what is happening. A drive, a pressure governs it; holding sway over the soul like a command: the desire and the will to fly away, anywhere, no matter what the cost: a violent, dangerous desire for an undiscovered world flares up and burns in all the senses. "Better to die than live *here*" howls the voice, even though this "here" is everything which it had hitherto loved! A sudden revulsion and suspicion at what it had loved; a lightning flash of scorn towards all obligations; a rebellious, despotic, volcanic hunger to roam across foreign territories; to become alienated, cold, sober: a hatred of love; an intoxicated inner shudder betraying a kind of victory – the *first* victory. This is also an affliction that can destroy a man, this will to *free* will – the magnitude of this disease is expressed in the wild gestures the freed man makes to prove his rule over things. He wanders abroad like a savage, he tears apart that which attracts him. With evil laughter he overturns what he finds hidden; he investigates how these things look if they are overturned. [HH]

One must travel a long way to the inner spaciousness and indulgence of a superabundance which precludes the danger that the spirit may get lost on some of its own pathways, fall in love, and stay where it is, intoxicated, curled up in a hole; a long way to the excess of healing, reviving powers, the sign of *great* health, the excess that confers upon the free spirit the dangerous privilege of being able to live experimentally and offer himself up to adventure. No longer ensnared in hatred or in love, one lives without Yes and No, voluntarily near and yet voluntarily distant; preferring to slip away, to avoid, to flutter on, flying upward, away. [HH]

All that we now need, something which can indeed only be given to us now, given the level of achievement of the various sciences, is a *chemistry* of moral, religious, aesthetic, ideas and feelings; a chemistry of all the drives that we experience in both the great and the small interactions of culture and society, and even in solitude. And what if this chemistry were to end in the conclusion that even the most glorious colours are derived from base, vulgar, even despised substances? Are there many who will have the courage to pursue such lines of investigation? Humanity loves to put all matters of origins and beginnings out of the question: consequently, must one not be almost inhuman to feel inclined towards the opposite? [HH]

Let us voice this new demand more clearly: we need a *critique* of moral values, *the inherent value of these values must be called into question.* The *value* of these "values" has hitherto been read as given, as factual, as completely unproblematic: no-one ever doubted or thought twice about assuming the "good man" to be of greater value than the "evil man" – greater in the sense of furthering the evolution and prosperity of man in general (including the future of man). But what if the reverse were true? What if a symptom of regression is intrinsic to "the good" – a danger, a seduction, a narcotic, by means of which the present *lives at the expense of the future?* – Then what if morality can be held responsible, if the highest power and wealth actually possible to man is never attained? What if morality is, precisely, the danger of dangers? [GM]

Since it is no longer feasible for man to believe that a God guides the fate of the world as a whole, or that, despite all apparent setbacks, the path taken by humanity leads inevitably to somewhere glorious, men set themselves various ecumenical goals embracing the entire earth. An older morality, that of Kant, requires from the individual those actions that one desires from all men – an amiable, naïve idea – assuming that, straight away and without further reflection, everyone would know what course of action would benefit the whole of humanity. This is a theory that resembles the theory of free trade, which assumes that a general equilibrium would necessarily result of itself, according to innate global laws of mediation. Maybe, in the future, a survey of all the needs of humanity will reveal that it is completely undesirable that all men act identically; and, on the contrary, in the pursuit of ecumenical goals, certain special tasks would have to be set – perhaps even evil ones.

If humanity is to be prevented from destroying itself with such a conscious, total government, we need to begin to research a *knowledge of the conditions of culture* as a scientific index for ecumenical goals. This is the overwhelming task for all the great minds of the next century. [HH]

That commanding thing which the people calls "spirit" desires to be master within itself and around itself, and it wants to *feel* its mastery: coming out of multiplicity, it possesses a will to simplicity, a will which binds things together and tames them, a will which is domineering and imperious. The power of the spirit to assimilate what is alien to it is revealed in a strong predisposition to appropriate the new to the old, to simplify that which is complex, to ignore or repulse all that which is totally contradictory – all at the same time as it capriciously emphasizes, extracts, and falsifies certain traits and lines in all that is alien to it, in every fragment of "external world", to suit itself. At the same time, this will is also served by what may appear to be an antithetical drive of the spirit, an instant decision to remain ignorant, to arbitrarily shut out, to close all the windows, to inwardly refuse this or that thing or even allow it to approach, a kind of defensive stance assumed against a great deal that *can* be known, to be content to hide in the dark, behind the closed horizon, to accept and approve of ignorance: all of this is necessary according to the power of the spirit to appropriate, according to (to speak metaphorically) its "digestive power". The spirit is more like a stomach than anything else. But here also belongs that intermittent will of the spirit to be deceived, perhaps with the mischievous idea that such and such a thing is *not* the case, that it is merely being allowed to pass for the case, a joy in all that is uncertain and ambiguous, an ecstatic enjoyment of all the arbitrary narrowness and concealment of a dark corner, of that which is all too close at hand, of the foreground, of the exaggerated, of the degraded, the displaced, the embellished, an enjoyment of the capricious nature of all these expressions of power. Finally there belongs here a not entirely innocent willingness of the spirit to deceive other spirits and dissemble before them; a continual pulsing and pressing of a formative, mutable force. In this the spirit is enraptured in the multiplicity and cunning of its masks. This will to simplification, recourse to the mask, to the cloak, to all that is superficial – is cancelled by that sublime disposition in a man of knowledge which takes a profound, multiple, and rigorous view of things, which *will* take such a view as a kind of cruelty inherent to the intellectual conscience. He will answer everything with: "There is something cruel in my spiritual inclinations" – and let us see the tractable and the virtuous seek to talk him out of that! But perhaps it would be better if we were credited with an "extravagant honesty" rather than with cruelty – we very free spirits – in the end, perhaps this may become our posthumous fame?

Until then – since this will not happen for a very long time – at least we are ill-disposed towards dressing ourselves up in moralistic verbal trimmings of this sort: honesty, love of truth, love of wisdom, sacrifice for truth, heroism of the truthful. We hermits have long been convinced that all this worthy verbal posturing belongs among the false adornments of old, the dead wood and fool's gold of unconscious human vanity, and that beneath these flattering colours and layers of polish, one can still make out the shape of that horrific basic script, *homo natura*. In order to translate man back into nature, in order to master the manifold vain, chimerical interpretations and secondary meanings which have been scribbled and splashed all over the eternal basic script, *homo natura*; in order to, from now on, confront man with himself in the way in which, hardened by the rigours of science, man has come to confront the rest of nature, with unflinching Oedipus eyes and blocked-up Odysseus ears, deaf to the siren songs of metaphysical bird catchers who, for far too long, have sought to seduce him by twittering: "You are more! You are higher! You have a different origin!" – may be a strange and excessive task. But who would deny that it *is* a task? [BGE]

Has the story with which the bible opens ever really been understood – the story of God's mortal terror in the face of science?.... Not yet. As is fitting, this priest's book begins with an account of the priest's greatest inner obstacle: he has only one danger, and, consequently, "God" also only has one great danger.

Old God, pure "spirit", almighty high-priestly perfection, potters around in his garden: but he gets bored. Against

62

boredom, even the gods fight in vain. So what does he do? He creates man – because man is entertaining. But what is to be done now? – man is also bored; and God's sympathy for the only kind of misery which creeps into every Paradise is limitless. Straight away, he creates other animals. This is God's first mistake, since man did not find the animals entertaining – he just dominated them, while refusing to become one of them. So God created Woman. And there, at last, was the end of boredom – and of a lot more besides! Woman was God's second mistake. "Woman is, in her essence, serpent," – every priest knows that; "every evil comes into the world through woman" – likewise. "Consequently science, too, comes into the world through her".... It was only through woman that man learned to taste the fruits of the tree of knowledge.

What had gone wrong? Old God was gripped by panic. Man himself had become God's *greatest* mistake! God had created for himself a potential enemy, since science makes man equal to God. Everything is over for priests and gods if man becomes a scientist! – Moral: science is, in itself, the pursuit of all that is forbidden – it alone is forbidden in the garden. Science is the first sin, the germ of all sins to come, the original sin.

"Thou shalt not know" – is the foundation of morality. Everything else follows. But God's fits of panic did not stop him from being shrewd. What defence can one have against science? Answer: expel man from Paradise! Happiness and idleness give room for thinking – and all thoughts are bad thoughts. Man *shall not think*. And so the "Priest in himself" invents misery, death, the threat to life in pregnancy, all kinds of despair, aging, toil, and, above all, sickness – all of which were weapons in the war against science! When a man is in distress, he has no opportunity to think!

But nevertheless, O horror! the structures of knowledge tower up, storming Heaven, assaulting the divine – what is to be done? – And so Old God invents war: he divides up the peoples, and provokes men to exterminate each other (priests have always needed to use war). War – amongst other things, it is a great cause of controversy in science! – What? Knowledge, liberation from the priest, population increases – all in spite of wars?

Old God comes to a final decision: "Man has become scientific – there is only one solution: he will have to be drowned!" [A]

All this "modern science" is the greatest ally of the ascetic ideal at present – and this is precisely because it is its most unconscious, involuntary, concealed, and underground ally! They have both been playing the same game up until now, the "paupers of the spirit" and the scientific opponents of this ideal (not the opposites of it, though). As for the famous "victories" of science, they *are* undoubtedly victories – but over what? The ascetic ideal has certainly not been destroyed: in fact, it has become stronger, which is to say, more slippery, more spiritual, more captious, as science rigorously broke down and demolished wall after wall of external appearances which had merely made its surface appear blemished. Who really believes that the defeat of theological astronomy constituted a defeat for that ideal?

Perhaps man has grown out of his need for transcendent answers to the riddle of existence – now that this existence appears to be more aleatory, impoverished, and thoroughly expendable in terms of the visible order of things? Since Copernicus, has it not been the case that the self-denigration of man, his *will to self-denigration*, has greatly gathered momentum? The faith which man once had in his singular importance, in his irreplaceability at the head of the great chain of being, is a thing of the past – he has become an animal: he who was once, according to his old faith, almost God ("child of God", "God man").

Ever since Copernicus, man has found himself on a slope – now he slips away, at ever increasing speed, down, away from the centre of the universe towards – what? Nothingness? – towards an all-pervading sense of his nothingness? Well then! – isn't this just the fast track to the old ideal?

All science (we by no means confine this to astronomy, about the degrading effects of which Kant made the remarkable confession: "it destroys my importance"), all science, whether natural or *unnatural* – (which is what I call the endless self-critique of knowledge) – still has the objective of destroying man's former self-respect, as if it was nothing but a strange conceit. One might go as far as to say that its own pride, its own form of stoical austerity, depends upon maintaining man's self-loathing at a constant level as a measure of his final and most serious claim to self-respect. Does this really militate against the ascetic ideal? Does anyone still really believe (as theologians used to imagine) that Kant's "victory" over all the dogmas of theology (i.e. "God", "soul", "freedom", "immortality") damaged that ideal in the slightest? – (It is no concern of ours, at the moment, to ask if Kant ever had any intention of doing this anyway!) – What can be proved is that, since Kant, transcendental minds of every kind have won the day – and they are no longer fettered by theology – what joy! Kant uncovered for them a secret path by means of which they are able, on their own initiative and with all scientific integrity intact, to follow their "heart's desire".

Who could hold it against these agnostics if, as acolytes of the unknown and the mysterious as such, they begin to worship the question mark as God? Through the presumption that everything that man "knows" not only fails to satisfy his desires, but actually negates them and produces a sense of horror, they gain a divine route to seek responsibility for this in "knowledge", and not desire!

"There is no knowledge: consequently there is a God" – new heights of elegance for the syllogism! What a victory for ascetic ideals! [GM]

Alas! To where can my longing now climb? From the top of every mountain I look out for fatherlands and motherlands.

But I have found a home nowhere; I am restless in all cities and I leave through every gate.

Modern men, towards whom my heart once drove me, seem strange to me – an absurdity; and I have been driven out of all fatherlands and motherlands.

Now I love only *the land of my children*, the uncharted land beyond the most distant ocean: I set my sails to seek it out.

I will compensate my children for being the children of my fathers: and compensate all the future – for *this* present! [Z]

O, my brothers: your nobility shall not gaze longingly backwards, but outwards! You shall be fugitives escaping from all fatherlands and motherlands!

You shall love the land of your children, and you shall compensate your children for being the children of your fathers: this is how you shall redeem all that is past! [Z]

Let where you are going, not where you came from, be your honour from this moment on! Let your new honour be your new will and your foot that will step out beyond you! [Z]

CHAPTER TWO

THE ECSTASY OF THE TRAGIC

1. THE BIRTH OF TRAGEDY

Here we see unveiled, perhaps for the first time, a kind of pessimism truly "beyond good and evil" – a philosophy which dares to dethrone morality and locate it in the phenomenal world: not only among the 'phenomena', the 'ideas', (in the strictly technical sense of these words when employed by idealists), but also among the 'deceptions', as illusion, as hallucination, as error, interpretation, artifice, art. [BT]

Hatred of this world, disparaging of the emotions, fear of sensual beauty and of sensuality, a transcendental world created in order to all the better heap slander upon this one – in short, a thirst for non-existence, a desire for sleep until the coming of the 'sabbath of all sabbaths' – all of these, along with the unswerving determination of Christianity to recognize only moral values, suddenly became for me the most dangerous and sinister manifestations of a 'will to decline'; or, at the very least, symptoms of the most intense affliction, fatigue, misery, exhaustion, impoverished life. For in the face of morality, especially unrestrained, Christian morality, life is necessarily always at fault, forever in the wrong, because life itself is essentially *amoral*. Crushed beneath the dead weight of self-loathing and eternal negation, life is necessarily felt to be undesirable, worthless in itself. My instinct, an instinct to affirm life, turned against morality in mobilizing a fundamentally opposing valuation of life, purely artistic and vehemently anti-Christian. As a philologist and a scholar, I named it, allowing myself a certain degree of licence – since who really knows the proper name of the Antichrist? – with the name of a Greek god: I named it *Dionysian*. [BT]

(Two Tendencies In Tragic Art: Apollonian And Dionysian)
In order to arrive at a better understanding of these two tendencies, we need only conceive of them first as the separate artistic worlds of dream and intoxication. [BT]

The seductive illusion of dream worlds, which every man is an accomplished artist in creating, is the precondition of any kind of visual art and of an important body of poetry. We take great pleasure in the sensual proximity of form, where all shapes speak to us, and nothing is listless or unnecessary. Nevertheless, even when this dream reality is manifested before us at the greatest pitch of intensity, we hold onto the impression, flitting in and out of consciousness, that it is still an *illusion*. [BT]

But it is not solely the case that pleasant and agreeable images are experienced by man with such a degree of universal comprehension: it is also true that the serious, the dark, the deeply sad, the most clasping restraints, the hideous mockeries of chance, in other words the whole "divine comedy" of life, including the Inferno, passes before his eyes – not only as in a shadowplay, since he himself lives and suffers through these scenes – but still he retains a fleeting sense of illusion, calling out to him among all the perils and horrors of the nightmare in encouragement: "It is a dream! I want to dream on!" [BT]

However, Schopenhauer has described the surging dread that washes over man when, all of a sudden, he loses his way among the cognitive forms of appearance, because the principle of sufficient reason, in some form or other, appears to have become unhinged. If we add to this panic the dreadful, blissful ecstasy awakened by this fragmentation of the *principium individuationis* (principle of individuation), which rises up from man's innermost core, which rises up from within nature itself, we are permitted a glimpse into the nature of the Dionysian – comprehensible to us, in the first instance, with reference to the analogy of intoxication. Animated by the narcotic potions sacred to primitive man, or by the ineluctable advance of spring, the Dionysian drives are awakened; and, as they gradually intensify, subjectivity becomes a complete forgetting of the self. There are some people who, either through a gap in their experience, or through simple-minded folly, recoil with pity and scorn from phenomena like these, dismissing them as 'folk diseases', fortified by an elevated sense of their own sanity. These impoverished creatures cannot know how diseased and ghostly this sanity they vaunt seems to be when the radiating life of Dionysian revellers thunders across their path. The slave becomes a free man, now that all the rigid and hostile borders, erected between man and man by fear, despotism, or mores, break down. The earth willingly offers up her gifts; the predatory beasts of the cliffs and the deserts placidly close in. [BT]

In all corners of the ancient world, from Rome to Babylon, we can verify the existence of Dionysian festivals. Almost without exception, the centre of these festivals was an abundant lack of sexual discipline, the crashing waves of which resonated across all the sanctified rules of family life. Here, the most savage beasts of nature were unfettered and let loose. [BT]

The terrible "witches' potion" of lust and cruelty thus unleashed gradually diminished in intensity, and only the peculiar emotional dualism of Dionysian revellers is able to recall it, as medicines are synthesized from deadly poisons – the experience of pain as joy, that jubilation which squeezes tormented screams out of the breast. At the moment of the highest joy we hear someone wailing in horror, or crying out in lament for something that has been lost, never to return. The Greek festivals illuminate a sentimental side of nature, as if she lamented her dissipation into individuals. [BT]

However, it would seem to be the case that, for quite some time, the Greeks were comprehensively sheltered and protected from the feverish excitations of these festivals by the figure of Apollo – which rose up in majestic pride, holding out the Gorgon's head to the grotesque, savage Dionysian, the most dangerous, catastrophic force with which it had to contend. [BT]

A Dionysian artist is thoroughly merged with the primal unity, with its pain and disjunction; and produces a mirror image of that primal unity as music, if we can truly call music a repetition and rebuilding of the world. Under the influence of the Apollonian dream, this music is revealed to him as an allegory – a dream-image. The reflection of ecstatic pain in sound, free of images and concepts, and moderated by illusion, goes on to create a second mirror image as a single allegory, or example. The artist abandons his subjectivity in the Dionysian process – but the image reveals to him his merging with the heart of the world in a dream scene which symbolizes the primal disjunction and pain, as well as the primal joy in illusion. The "I" of the lyric poet bursts forth from the depths of his being. He loses himself in the pure contemplation of images. [BT]

Inasmuch as he interprets music by means of images, he lies floating on the lapping waves of Apollonian contemplation, even though all that he accesses through the medium of music may be in urgent, compulsive motion. If he sees himself through the same medium, he glimpses the image of himself in a state of unsatisfied emotion: his own desire, his yearning, his groans, and his cries of joy become a symbol through which he interprets music for himself. This is the phenomenon of the lyric poet: an Apollonian genius, he interprets music by means of the image of the will. [BT]

Nevertheless, there is nothing ascetic about all this, nothing which suggests spirituality or duty – everything attests to an abundant and triumphant existence, in which everything is held to be sacred, regardless of whether it is good or evil. [BT]

The old story goes like this – King Midas, for a long time, had hunted the wise satyr, Silenus, the companion of Dionysus, but had failed to catch him. When Silenus finally fell into his hands, the king asked him what was the best and most desirable thing to strive for. The demon stood still, rigid and silent, until finally, compelled by the king, he emitted a shrill burst of laughter and answered thus: "Miserable, fleeting race; children of danger and suffering; why do you compel me to say what it would be better for you never to hear? The best thing of all is something completely beyond your grasp: never to have been born, not to be, to be nothing. However, the second best thing, for you at least, is to die soon." [BT]

The Greeks knew and felt all the panic and horror of existence: in order for them to live at all they had to insert the scintillating dream-birth of the Olympian gods between themselves and these horrors. We might sketch their origin in the following: the Apollonian impulse towards beauty transformed the old Titanic order of gods of fear into the Olympian gods of joy, in the same way that roses open on thorn bushes. [BT]

An existence bathed in the shimmering sunlight of gods like these was felt to be the highest goal of mankind, and true grief was experienced at the thought of leaving it, especially when that departure was close at hand. It might well be necessary to reverse the wisdom of Silenus to say: "The worst thing of all would be to die soon, the second worst would be to die at all." [BT]

The Dionysian state of ecstasy, which abolishes the normal thresholds and borders of existence, actually contains, throughout its duration, a lethargic element which engulfs all past experience. By means of this chasm of oblivion, the separation of the mundane and Dionysian realities is consolidated. But the more one becomes aware of this mundane reality, the more repellent it becomes – it leads to an ascetic mood, a denial of the will. Dionysian man shares this affect with Hamlet: both have seen into the very essence of things, they have understood, and are repelled by the thought of action: since no action of theirs can change anything of the eternal essence of things, and they consider it absurd, or even shameful, to be expected to be able to generate order in a world of chaos. Understanding destroys action, and action depends upon a veil of illusion: this is what we learn from Hamlet – but not the common interpretation of Hamlet as a daydreamer who, as a result of an excess of reflection upon a manifold of possibilities, fails to act. Not reflection! Not that! – A deep understanding, an insight into the horrific truth, is what counterweights every motive for action for both Hamlet and the Dionysian man. No consolation of order will be of any use from here on in: longing passes out of the world towards death, beyond the gods, beyond existence which, whether reflected by the gods or expressed in the thought of an immortal "Beyond", is denied. Suddenly conscious of the truth from a brief glimpse of it, all man sees is the full horror and absurdity of his existence. Now he will understand the symbolism of the fate of Ophelia – now he will understand the wisdom of Silenus: and it repels him.

Here, with the will in supreme danger, there comes a redeeming, healing enchantress – art. It is she alone who is capable of transforming all these feelings of revulsion at the horror and absurdity of existence into ideas which are compatible with the continuation of life. These are the sublime (or the domestication of horror by means of art); and comedy (the artistic discharge from the revulsion of absurdity). [BT]

Apollo appears to us as the apotheosis of the *principium individuationis*. Apollo, considered as an ethical god, commands moderation from his followers, coupled with self-knowledge in order to maintain it. Thus the admonitions "know thyself" and "nothing to excess" coexist with the aesthetic necessity of beauty; while, on the other hand, hubris and excess are considered to be malign spirits of the extra-Apollonian realm; qualities of the age of the Titans, of the world of the barbarians. [BT]

But the Apollonian Greeks were also unable to hide from the fact that they were themselves intimately related to those fallen Titans and heroes. They were forced even deeper into the core of their being – their whole existence, all its beauty and moderation notwithstanding, was based upon a veiled substratum of suffering and knowledge, revealed to them once again by the Dionysian. Behold! Apollo could not live without Dionysus! [BT]

The individual, with all his self-control, restraints, and moderation, became submerged in the self-extinction of the Dionysian state, and became oblivious to all the Apollonian dictates. Excess was unveiled as truth, contradiction, and the ecstasy born of pain raised its voice from the heart of nature. The consequence of this was that wherever the Dionysian invasion was successful, the Apollonian was negated and abolished. [BT]

The inspired worshipper of Dionysus does nothing more then feel; he does not condense into an image. [BT]

The Dionysian celebrant sees himself as a satyr, and it is as a satyr that he looks upon his god. In this transformation he looks upon a new vision outside himself, the Apollonian complement of his state. In the light of this, we need to see Greek tragedy as a Dionysian chorus continually discharging its energies in an Apollonian world of images. [BT]

If we make a determined effort to stare into the heart of the sun and turn away blinded, we see dark-coloured patches before our eyes, acting as what we might call remedies. The light-image manifestations of the Apollonian mask are the inevitable products of a momentary gaze into the terrifying core of nature: light patches to heal the wounded gaze scorched by terrible night. [BT]

Dionysus is manifested in a multiplicity of forms; in the mask of a warrior-hero and, it might be said, captured in the net of the individual will. As the god speaks and acts on stage, he comes to look like an erring, determined, suffering individual – and the fact that he appears with any of this precision and clarity is the effect of Apollo, the interpreter of dreams, who reveals the Dionysian state of the chorus through this symbolic appearance. However, this hero is also the suffering Dionysus of the mysteries – the god who, as fantastic myths relate, was dismembered by the Titans and was, in that condition, worshipped as Zagreus. This means that the true Dionysian suffering, dismemberment, amounts to a transformation into air, water, earth, and fire; and that we should therefore see the state of individuation as the source and origin of all suffering, and, as such, something entirely reprehensible. The Olympian gods were born from the smile of Dionysus, humanity from his tears. Existing as a dismembered god, Dionysus presented the dual aspect of cruel, savage demon, and mild, benevolent ruler. The hope of the epopts was the *rebirth* of Dionysus, which we can interpret, not without some distant rumbling of dread, as the end of individuation: the epopts' deafening hymn to joy celebrated the coming of this third Dionysus. This single hope is all that beams a ray of joy across the face of the world, torn-up and fragmented into individuals, and mythically symbolized by Demeter, sunk down in eternal sorrow, who is only able to rejoice again when told that she may give birth to Dionysus once more. [BT]

Let us consider how after Socrates, the mystagogue of science, wave upon wave of new philosophical schools emerged and then disappeared; how a desire for knowledge unknown up until this point throughout the whole of the educated world led science onto the high seas from which it has never been entirely expelled; how this new universality first established a common network of rational thought across the world, allowing a glimpse into the law-bound operation of an entire solar system. As soon as we recognize this as the base of the incredibly high pyramid of knowledge of the present day, we are compelled to see in Socrates the break, the vortex of world history. If we imagine what might have happened if that immeasurable wealth of energy expended in that global tendency had been used in ways not serving knowledge, but in ways attached to the practical, selfish goals of individuals and states, universal wars of annihilation and endless migration of peoples would have weakened man's instinctive joy in living to the point where, suicide having become universal, the individual would feel it his duty as a son to throttle his parents, or, as a friend, his friend, as the islanders of Fiji do: a practical pessimism that could escalate so far as to produce a horrific ethic of genocide through pity. [BT]

It is thus that the Apollonian wrenches us out of Dionysian universality. With the tremendous impact of images, concepts, ethical teachings, and stirrings of sympathy, the Apollonian lifts man out of this orgiastic self-destruction. [BT]

But what hopes awaken when we see signs of the re-awakening of the Dionysian spirit in our contemporary world! Out of the Dionysian earth of the German spirit, a power has sprung forth that has nothing to do with all these conditions for Socratic culture. That kind of culture cannot explain this, and neither can it ignore it: it finds it terrifying, enigmatic, powerful, hostile. It is *German music* in its mighty solar cycle running from Bach to Beethoven, and from Beethoven to Wagner. How can the knowledge-hungry Socratism of our own times possibly deal with this demon rising from the abyss? Everything that we now refer to as culture, education, and civilization will one day kneel before that infallible judge, Dionysus.

We need only recall how, through Kant and Schopenhauer, the spirit of German philosophy, flowing out of the same wellspring, destroyed the smug delight in existence of Socratism by revealing its limitations, and thus introduced a far more profound and serious questioning of art and ethics – a formation which we might be tempted to describe as Dionysian wisdom in a conceptual form. For to where does the mystery of the union of German music and German philosophy beckon, if not towards a new mode of existence which we can only access by means of Greek analogies? As we do this, we sense the birth of a new tragic age in the German spirit – signifying a return to itself, a joyful self-rediscovery, which can learn only from a single nation: from the Greeks. [BT]

What changes drift across the weary desert of our culture when it is stirred by the magic of Dionysus! A storm rages against everything that is decrepit, decaying, broken, stunted; it smothers it all in a whirlwind of red dust, and carries it off into the sky like a vulture. Confused and vain, we grasp after all that has disappeared; because what we can see has risen, as if it came from beneath the earth, into the gold light, full and green, vigorously alive, immeasurable, filled with desire. Tragedy is enthroned in sublime rapture in the middle of this abundance of life, pain, and joy, listening to a distant, melancholy song which hymns all the Mothers of Being – Delusion, Will, and Sorrow.

Join me, my friends, in my faith in a Dionysian life and the rebirth of tragedy. The Socratic age is over. Put on a crown of ivy, hold onto the thyrsus, and do not be surprised if tigers and panthers timidly lie down at your feet. Dare to be men of the tragic – for you will find redemption there! [BT]

2. DIONYSUS RECONFIGURED

(On the "Birth Of Tragedy"): I now regret that I did not possess the courage (or the audacity?) to permit myself to formulate a new language in keeping with those new insights and dangerous ideas of mine – that I laboured through it all using Schopenhauerian and Kantian concepts to express a strange, new kind of evaluation fundamentally at odds with the spirit and taste of Kant and Schopenhauer! In the end, what was Schopenhauer's view of the tragic? In the second volume of his "World As Will And Representation", he writes: *"What gives all that is tragic, whatever its form, a characteristic of the sublime, is the first inkling of the knowledge that the world and life can give no true satisfaction, and are not worth our investment in them. The tragic spirit consists in this. Accordingly, it leads to resignation."* But, O, Dionysus spoke otherwise to me! – Even then I was far beyond this kind of resignation! I regret that I botched the grandiose Greek problem by grafting onto it the most modern ideas, introducing hopes where there was no hope, where everything pointed towards an ending. I regret that I began to hymn the "German spirit", on the basis of the most recent German music (i.e. that of Wagner), as if it were at the point of rediscovering and reformulating itself – at the very time when the German spirit, on the pathetic pretext of empire-building, was making a gradual transition to mediocrity. Since then, I have learned to think about that "German spirit" without hope or pity – and, in the same way, about modern German music, which is completely romantic: of all possible art forms it is the one that is *least Greek*. It is also a narcotic of the worst kind, particularly dangerous for a people who love intoxication so much – which raises lack of clarity to the level of a virtue, with its double narcotic effect of intoxication and numbness. But, apart from all the precocious hopes for, and transpositions of, contemporary issues which ruined my first book, the great Dionysian question mark remains: what would it be like – a music that was not romantic in origin, like German music, but Dionysian? [BT – "Attempt At Self-Criticism"]

I was the first to notice the real opposition: the declining instinct that turns against life in a subterranean desire for revenge (Christianity, the philosophy of Schopenhauer, all forms of idealism) against a formula for the highest affirmation of life – born out of abundance, out of over-abundance, an unreserved affirmation, even of suffering, even of guilt, even of everything questionable and alien in existence.

This ultimate, joyous, luxurious "Yes" to life represents the highest and the deepest insight; all that which is most rigorously confirmed by truth and science. Nothing may be subtracted from existence, nothing is expendable – all the aspects of life condemned by Christians and other nihilists are actually of an infinitely higher order than the order of rank of values that the instinct of decadence could affirm and call good. It takes courage to understand this, and, as a precondition for this, an excess of strength: it is by means of this measure of strength that courage ventures out as far forwards as it can possibly go, and begins to approach truth. Knowledge, the affirmation of reality, is as necessary for the strong as cowardice and fleeing from reality, the "ideal", is for the weak, who are driven by weakness. [EH]

It is because of this that I have the right to think of myself as the first tragic philosopher – the most vehement enemy and opposite of a pessimistic philosopher. Before me this transformation of the Dionysian into a kind of philosophical pathos had not taken place: tragic wisdom was absent; I searched in vain for the merest signs of it, even among the great minds of Greek philosophy, i.e. those of the pre-Socratics. I harboured some doubts in the case of Heraclitus, the company of whom makes me feel warmer and better than that of anyone else. The affirmation of passing away and destruction, which is the most important feature of a Dionysian philosophy; saying Yes to antipathy and war; *becoming* set alongside a radical negation of the concept of being – all of this is closer to me than any other kind of thought to date. The doctrine of the Eternal Return; the unconditional, infinitely recurring, circular movement of all things might in the end have been taught by Heraclitus. Even the Stoics show traces of it – and they inherited most of their principal notions from Heraclitus.[1] [EH]

What Is Romanticism?

Any kind of art, any kind of philosophy, can be regarded as a remedy and aid put to the service of a growing, struggling life – both always presuppose the existence of suffering and sufferers. This being said, there are two kinds of sufferers: firstly, there are those who suffer from *over-abundance of life* – these people want a Dionysian art coupled with a tragic view of life, a tragic insight – and then, secondly, there are those who suffer from *impoverishment of life*, who crave rest, stillness, untroubled waters, redemption from themselves through art, or knowledge, or intoxication, or convulsions, or anaesthesia, or insanity. All artistic romanticism complies with the needs of the latter kind; and that includes Schopenhauer as well as Richard Wagner, to mention the names of the two most famous and prominent romantics whom I once *misunderstood* – not, by the way, to their disadvantage at the time. The man that is the richest in the abundance of life, the Dionysian god and man, is not only able to afford to countenance the sight of all that is fearful and questionable but also the fearful act and any luxury of destruction, disintegration, and negation. In his case, all that is evil, irrational, and ugly seems tolerable owing to an excess of procreating, fertilizing energies capable of

---

1: The affinity Nietzsche experiences in the proximity of "dark Heraclitus" should become obvious from these fragments (c.5th Century B.C.): (i) "War is the father of all and king of all; and some he has shown as gods, others as men; some he has made slaves, others free." (ii) "The way up and down is one and the same." (iii) "Man's character is his fate." (iv) "Graspings: wholes and not wholes, convergent divergent, consonant dissonant, from all things one and from one thing all." (v) "There is a Great Year, whose winter is a great flood and whose summer is a world conflagration. In these alternating periods the world is now going up in flames, now turning to water. This cycle consists of 10,800 years." (Source: Charles H. Kahn: *The Art And Thought Of Heraclitus*.)

---

turning any desert into verdant pastures. On the other hand, those who suffer most and lead the most impoverished lives, more than anything else, would need mildness, tranquillity, and goodness in their thoughts and in their acts – and, if possible, a god who would be a god providing comfort for the sick, a healer, a saviour; along with logic, the conceptual delimitation of existence – since logic calms and bestows confidence – in short, a certain kind of warm constriction that holds fear at a distance and envelops the sufferer in optimistic horizons.

It is thus that I gradually learned to understand Epicurus, the reverse of a Dionysian pessimist; and also the "Christian", who is no more than another kind of Epicurean – both are fundamentally romantics – and my eye grew ever sharper in observing that most difficult and fractious form of *reverse inference* through which the largest number of mistakes are made: the reverse inference from the product to the producer, from the deed to the doer, from the ideal to the people who need it, from every line of thinking and valuing to the commanding need behind it.

With regard to all aesthetic values, I now avail myself of this major distinction: in every case, I ask: "Is it hunger or over-abundance that has become creative?" In the first instance, a different distinction might seem preferable, one which is far more obvious – the question of whether the desire to immobilize, to immortalize, the desire for *being* impelled creation; or the desire for destruction, for change, for the future, for becoming. But, if scrutinized closely, both of these kinds of desire will be seen to be ambiguous. They can both be interpreted with reference to the first scheme, which seems to me to be preferable. Desire for destruction, change, and becoming can be an expression of an over-flowing energy which is pregnant with the future (my term for this is

"Dionysian"); but, nevertheless, it can also express the hatred of the ill-constituted, the disowned, the impoverished; who destroy, who *must destroy*, because everything that exists, even existence itself, infuriates and provokes them. In order to comprehend this feeling, scrutinize our anarchists closely.

The will to *immortalize* also demands a dual interpretation. First, it can be prompted by gratitude and love. Art originating from this will always be an art of apotheoses, beaming light and glory over all things. But it can also express the autocratic will of one who suffers to the very core, who struggles, who is tormented, and who desires to convert all that which is most singular, personal, and constricting, the real perversity of his suffering, into a binding law and a compulsion – one who revenges himself on all things by burning his own image into them, the image of his own torture. This is *romantic pessimism* in its most accomplished form, whether it be found in Schopenhauer's philosophy of the will, or in Wagner's music – romantic pessimism, the final *great* event in the fate of our culture.

(That it would still be possible for there to be a completely different kind of pessimism, a classical type: this insight and vision belongs entirely to me, is inseparable from me; only the word "classical" is offensive to my ear – I call this pessimism of the future; for it is coming! I can see it coming! Dionysian pessimism.) [GS]

This is my rapture: to stand up above everything like its own sky, like its circular roof, its azure bell and eternal certainty.

All things are anointed in the fount of eternity. They are all beyond good and evil. And good and evil are, themselves, merely interloping shadows, damp afflictions, passing clouds.

It is a consecration and not a blasphemy when I tell you that over all things arch the heavens of chance, the heavens of innocence, the heavens of fortuity, the heavens of abandonment.

Chance is the world's most ancient nobility – it is to this that I have returned all things. I have unleashed them all from their submission to purpose.

I set this freedom and cosmic cheerfulness in motion, ringing out over all things like an azure bell, when I taught that there is no "eternal will" acting on and through them.

I set this abandonment and foolishness in the place of that eternal will when I taught: "Only one thing is impossible with all things – rationality!"

A little rationality is no doubt possible, seeds of reason scattered among the stars; but in all things I have found this happy certainty: they would rather dance – they would rather dance with feet of chance.

O, pure, regal sky up above me! This is your purity to me: there is no eternal spider of reason nor spider's web in you – to me you are a dance floor for sacred chance, a gods' table for sacred dice and dice players! [Z]

Apollonian intoxication above all excites the eye, with the result that it acquires power of vision. The painter, the sculptor, the epic poet, are visionaries *par excellence*. In the Dionysian state, the whole emotional system is affected and intensified: with the result that it discharges all its powers of representation, imitation, transformation, transmutation, all kinds of mimicry and role-playing at the same time. The essential thing is the facility of the metamorphosis, the inability *not* to react. It is impossible for the Dionysian man not to comprehend any suggestion, no matter what kind; he ignores no signal from the emotions, he possesses the instinct for comprehending and divining to the highest degree, and he is a master of the art of communication. He slips easily into every skin, into every emotion; he continually transforms himself. [TI]

Deception is everything
In times of war:
The skin of a fox
Shall be my secret suit of armour. [PF]

My formula for greatness in a human being is *amor fati* (love of fate): the notion that one would have nothing be otherwise than it is; not forwards, not backwards, not in all eternity. Not merely to bear what it is necessary to bear, and even less hide it away behind something – all idealism is mendaciousness in the face of all that is necessary – but *learn to love it.* [EH]

I have become tired of all poets, old and new: to me they all seem to be shallow and superficial seas.

They have never thought deeply enough: for that reason their feelings have never probed their depths.

A slight degree of sensuousness and a little boredom: that is all that their best ideas have ever amounted to.

The noise of all their harps sounds to me like so much coughing and gasping of ghosts – what have they ever known about the intensity of music?

And neither are they clean enough for me: they all agitate their waters in order to appear deep.

And it is like this that they strive to reveal themselves to be reconcilers: but, nevertheless, they still seem to me to be mere mediators, interferers, mediocre and filthy men!

Once I cast my net into their ocean waters, hoping to land some fine fish. But all I ever pulled out was the head of an old, dead god. [Z]

Once I wanted to dance like I had never danced before: I wanted to dance beyond all heavens. But they lured my favourite singer away from me.

And he began to play a grotesque, doleful melody – he roared in my ears like a mournful trumpet!

Murderous singer! Instrument of malice! Most innocent man! I stood poised to dance the most exquisite dance: and then my ecstasy was murdered by your cacophony!

My highest hope remains silent and unattained! All the visions and solace of my youth lie dead!

How did I bear it? How did I heal wounds like these, how did I overcome them? How was it that my soul rose once more and left these graves? [Z]

I am a handhold beside the stream: let him who is capable grasp me. However: I am not your crutch! [Z]

Have I been understood? – *Dionysus against the Crucified.* [EH]

CHAPTER THREE

WILL TO POWER 1:
SELF-OVERCOMING

I teach you the Overman. Man is something that ought to be overcome. What have you done to overcome him?

All creatures create something beyond themselves: would you prefer to become the ebb of this great flow, and slide back into bestiality than overcome Man?

What is an ape to mankind? Either a bad joke or a cause of bitter shame. And this is what Man shall be for the Overman: a bad joke or a cause of bitter shame.

You may have travelled far along the pathway from worm to man, but there is still much in you of the nature of worms. Once you were apes, but now man is more simian than any ape.

Even the wisest among you is nothing more than a

hermaphroditic hybrid of plant and ghost. Do I urge you to become plants or ghosts?

Behold! I teach you the Overman!

The Overman is the meaning of the Earth. Let your will speak thus: the Overman *shall* be the meaning of the Earth.

I implore you, my brothers, remain true to the Earth and do not believe in anyone who speaks to you of unearthly, supernatural hopes.

These people are despisers of life; atrophying and poisoned to the core. The Earth has grown weary of them: let them leave it soon !

Truly, man is a river of filth. One must be like an ocean to be able to receive a river of filth without being contaminated by it.

Behold! I teach you the Overman – he is this ocean: in him your great loathing can drown. [Z]

Man is a tightrope, stretching between animal and Overman – a tightrope over an abyss.

There is danger in going across, danger on the way, danger in looking back, danger in standing still and shuddering.

What is great in Man is that he is a bridge and not a destination: what can be loved in Man is that he goes across and goes under.

I love those who do not know how to live unless their life be a going-under, for they are the ones who are going across.

I love the great despisers – because they are great venerators and arrows of longing for different shores.

I love all those who do not first seek beyond the stars for a place to go under and become a sacrifice, but sacrifice themselves to the Earth – so that the Earth might one day belong to the Overman.

I love him who labours and invents in order to build a house for the Overman, and prepares the Earth, plants, and animals for him: for it is thus that he wills his own demise.

I love him who squanders his soul, who asks for no thanks and accepts nothing in return: because he always gives and does not preserve himself.

I love him who is ashamed when the dice fall in his favour, and then asks: "Am I, then, a cheat?" – because he wants to fall.

I love him who justifies the men of the future and redeems the men of the past: because he wants to die at the hands of the men of the present. [Z]

A multitude of suns orbit in empty space: they speak with their light to all that is dark. To me they remain silent.

O, this is the repulsion of light for that which emits light: it journeys unsparingly on its way.

Every sun travels like this – unjust to that which emits light in its deepest heart, cold towards all suns.

The suns hurtle along their courses like storms; that is their journey. They follow their unswerving will; that is their coldness.

O, it is only you, you shadowy, dark ones, who know how to extract warmth from light-givers! O, it is only you who drink milk and comfort from udders of light!

O, ice surrounds me, my hands are burned by ice!

Night comes: O, that I have to be light! That I must thirst for the things of night! For solitude! [Z]

Surveying the many refined and coarse moralities which have ruled, or still rule on earth I discovered certain traits which regularly recur together and are bound up together: at last, two basic types and a basic distinction between them emerged. There is *master morality* and *slave morality* – though to this I would add the immediate qualification that, in all higher and mixed cultures, attempts to mediate between the two are evident, as is confusion and mutual incomprehension between them, sometimes even their dissonant juxtaposition – even within the same man, within a *single* soul. These systems of moral evaluation have arisen out of a ruling order which was joyously aware of its distinction from the ruled – or from among the ruled: from among slaves and dependants of every station. When the rulers determine the value of the concept "good" it is exalted, proud states which are considered to be differentiating. These determine the order of rank. The noble human being distances himself from all natures in which the reverse of such exalted, proud states find expression: he despises them. At this juncture, it should be noted that in this first type of morality the antithesis "good" and "bad" is synonymous with the opposition "noble" and "despicable" – the antithesis "good" and "evil" originates elsewhere. The noble type of man feels *himself* to be the evaluator of values, he does not seek the approval of anyone, he judges that "that which harms me is harmful in itself," he knows himself to be someone who, in general, honours things: he *creates values.* He honours all that which he knows to be a part of himself – a morality of self-glorification. The feeling of plenitude stands in the foreground, the feeling of power seeking to overflow, the feeling of happiness in high tension, the consciousness of a luxurious wealth which would like to expend itself and give itself away – the noble human being even helps the unfortunate but not, or in any event almost not, from pity; but more from an urge emerging from superfluous strength. The noble human being honours the man of power in himself, the man who has power over himself, who knows how to speak and how to remain silent, who enjoys practising severity and harshness upon himself and reveres everything severe and harsh.

All this is otherwise in the second type of morality, *slave morality.* Supposing that the abused, the oppressed, the suffering, the bound, those uncertain of themselves and exhausted were to moralize: what would their evaluations of morals hold in common? [BGE]

Here is the source of the famous antithesis "good" and "evil" – power and danger were felt to lie at the heart of evil; a certain fearfulness, insidiousness and strength too great to inspire contempt. Thus, according to slave morality, "the evil" inspire fear; whereas, for master morality, it is "the good" who inspire fear – who *want* to inspire fear – while the "bad" man is judged to be despicable. The antithesis reaches its peak when a whisper of disdain comes to be attached to the "good" of this morality – a slight and benevolent disdain – because, within the slaves' mode of evaluation, the good man must always be a *harmless* man: good-natured, easily deceived, perhaps even a little stupid, *un bonhomme.* [BGE]

Until now all psychology has remained fastened to moral prejudices and inhibitions: it has never dared to explore the depths. To conceive of it as I do – as the morphology and development theory of the will to power – has so far not even occurred to anyone else: inasmuch as it can be permitted to view everything written before as a symptom of all that which has been kept silent. The power of moral prejudice has punctured deeply into the most spiritual world, which is apparently the coldest and most freely held of presuppositions – and, it goes without saying, has functioned there in a harmful, inhibiting, blinding, twisting fashion. A genuine physiological psychology needs to struggle against unconscious resistance in the experimenter, since "the heart" stands against it: to even postulate a theory of the interdependence of the "good" and "evil" impulses would trigger revulsion in a conscience remaining strong and hearty, as a newly refined immorality – and this is even more so for a theory of the derivation of all good impulses from evil ones. Let us suppose that someone goes so far as to view the emotions of hatred, jealousy, greed, and lust for domination as life-conditioning emotions; as things which must fundamentally and necessarily be present in the general economy of life, and which must be intensified if life itself is to be maintained – he would suffer from such a judgement as he would suffer from seasickness. Even this is still far from being the strangest and most painful insight in this immense and virtually unexplored domain of dangerous knowledge – in fact there are a hundred good reasons why everyone who can keep away from it – *should!* But then again, if your ship has been driven into these waters, very well! Now grit your teeth! Keep your eyes open! Hold on tightly to the helm! – We sail straight over morality and *beyond* it, we flatten it out; and perhaps we crush what remains of our own morality by daring to voyage out there – *but what do we matter?* [BGE]

Any philosopher who has ridden through many states of health, and continues to ride through them, has passed through an equally multiple number of philosophies; it is not possible for him to prevent himself from transmuting his states into the most spiritual form: philosophy consists, precisely, of this art of transmutation. We philosophers cannot allow ourselves to divide body and soul, as the people do; and we can allow ourselves to divide soul from spirit even less readily. We are not thinking frogs, nor objectifying and verifying mechanisms with their organs removed: in a constant process, we are forced to give birth to our thoughts out of pain and, like their mothers, invest them with all we have of blood, heart, fire, pleasure, passion, searing pain, conscience, fate, catastrophe. Life – that means for us a constant transformation of all that we have into light and flame, including everything that inflicts wounds upon us: there is nothing else we can do. As for great sickness – is it not true that we are tempted to ask whether we could live without it?

Only great pain, protracted, dragging pain that stretches out time – pain on whose pyre we are burned with green wood – forces us to sink down into our ultimate depths and to look away from all trust, everything good-natured, everything that lurks veiled, everything mild, everything mediocre – everything in which, in the past, we may have found our humanity. It is not that pains such as these make us "better" – what I do know is that they make us more *profound*.

Whether we learn to set our pride, our contempt, our will to power against it, in the same way as the American Indian who, tortured without relief, pays back his torturer with the scornful lash of his tongue; or whether we retreat from pain into that Oriental Nothingness – called Nirvana – into silent, rigid, deaf resignation, self-forgetting, self-destruction: one emerges as a different person after such protracted and dangerous exercises of self-mastery, possessing a few more question marks – more than anything else, possessing the will to question further, deeper, far more mercilessly, harshly, evilly, and quietly than one had ever questioned before. Trust in life is no longer enough: life itself becomes a *problem*. But still, one should not too readily assume that this necessarily makes one gloomy. Love of life is still possible, the only difference being that one loves it in a different way. It is love for a woman that causes us to doubt her.

The attraction of all that is unsettled, the delight in some x, is so great in such spiritual, spiritualized men that this rapture flares up over and over again, like a luminous blaze, over all the pain of what is problematic, over all the perils of uncertainty, and even over the lover's jealousy. We come to know a new happiness. [GS]

The Wanderer
The man who has only yet partially arrived at a freedom of reason cannot relate to this earth as anything but a wanderer – although not as a traveller turning his eyes towards a final goal in the distance, because there is no such thing. He desires to look around him, to keep his eyes open to everything that actually occurs in the world; and, therefore, he must not bind his heart too tightly to any single thing; there must always be something inside him that wanders, that takes its joy in all that changes, in all that is transitory. No doubt a man such as this will suffer bad nights; nights when, exhausted, he finds the gates to the city that should offer him rest closed. Perhaps the desert spreads all the way up to the gate, just as it does in the Orient, and the howls of beasts of prey can be heard, at first close at hand, and then far in the distance; perhaps a strong wind gathers, and robbers make off with his pack-animals. In this hour, the horrors of the night sink over the desert like a second desert, and his heart tires of wandering. And if the

morning sun should then rise, blazing like a god of revenge, and the gates of the city are opened, he may see even more of the desert in the faces of its people – more dirt, more deception, more confusion than outside the gates: the days drag on worse than the nights. Come as all this may, the ecstatic sunrises of other zones and days will come to the wanderer as a recompense. In the light of the dawn he sees bands of muses dancing around him through the mist of the mountains. He strolls quietly beneath trees, from whose high and leafy branches only worthwhile and bright things are showered upon him – the gifts of all those free spirits who are equally at home in the mountains, in the forests, in solitude; those who, like him, in their sometimes cheerful, sometimes sombre way, are wanderers and philosophers. [HH]

Do you presume yourself to be free? If so, then I want you to tell me what is your ruling idea, and not that you have broken free of some fetter.

Are you the kind of man who ought to be unfettered? For there are many who cast off their final value when they cast away their chains.

Free *from* what? I care nothing for that! I want to see this clearly in your eyes: free for what?

Are you able to endow yourself with your own good and your own evil? To suspend your own will over your head as a law? To be your own judge, and the avenger of your law?

To be alone with the judge and avenger of your own law is a terrifying thing. It is like the orbit of a lone star, hurled out into deep space, touched by the arctic cold of solitude.

O, man alone with himself: for the moment you may still from the many – for the moment you are still brimming with courage and hope.

But a day will come when solitude will drain your strength, a day when your pride will bend and your courage will snap. A day will come when you will howl: "I am alone!"

A day will come when you no longer see what is exalted about you; a day when you will see all too clearly what is loathsome about you; your elevated nature itself will plunge you into terror, as though it was a ghost. A day will come when you will howl: "All is false!"

These are the emotions that hunt the solitary down; and if they should fail – well, then, they must themselves be killed! Are you capable of becoming a murderer?

You force many to alter their opinions of you. They hold this against you. You veered closely towards them, but still went on your way past them: for this you will never be forgiven.

You go on up and beyond them: but the higher you climb, the smaller you appear to the eye of envy. More than this, he who can fly is hated most of all.

But the most formidable enemy you will ever encounter will be yourself; you lie in ambush for yourself, lurking in caves and forests.

You travel the road to yourself, solitary man! And your road leads past yourself and your seven devils!

To yourself you will be all these things – a heretic, a witch and a prophet; a sinner and a criminal.

You must be ready to incinerate yourself in your own flame – how could you become anew if you did not first wither into ashes?

You travel along the road of the lover: you love yourself and, for the same reason, you hate yourself as only lovers can hate. For what would he who has had no cause to hate what he loved know of love? [Z]

There are few set up to achieve autonomy – it is a privilege of the strong. And he who attempts to reach it, maybe having a complete *right* to do so, but without being *compelled* towards it, demonstrates that he is quite probably not only strong but also fearless to the point of recklessness. He plunges into a labyrinth, he multiplies by a thousand the dangers attendant upon such a life, not the least of which is that no-one is any longer able to perceive exactly how and where he has become lost, is cut off from others; is torn apart, limb from limb, by some minotaur lurking in a cave of conscience. If such a man is destroyed, this happens so far beyond the comprehension of men that they can neither feel it nor sympathize – and he can no longer go back! He can no longer go back – not even to the pity of men! [BGE]

This is your entire will, all you wise men, it is a will to power – and it is this even when you speak of good and evil and the evaluation of values.

You want to create a world before which you will kneel: this is your ultimate hope and your intoxication.

To be sure, the uninformed, the people, are like a river with a boat coursing down its stream. In this boat, sombre and disguised, sit the evaluations of values.

You set afloat your will and your values upon the river of becoming. What the people believe to be good and evil always masks this ancient will to power.

Now the river carries your boat along: it is compelled to carry it. It matters little if breaking waves crash and angrily oppose its boughs.

It is not in the river that your danger lies and the end of your good and evil; it is in that will itself, the will to power, the insatiable, fecundating will of life.

To command is more difficult than to obey – not only because the commander carries the weight of all those who obey him, but because this weight can so easily crush him.

It seems to me that in all commanding there is an experiment and a risk: the living creature always risks itself when it commands.

What is sacred to the greatest is to confront risk and danger, and play dice with death.

And life itself whispered this secret to me : "I am that which must overcome itself over and over again.

"You may call this a will to reproduce, or progress towards some goal, something higher, more distant, more multifarious: all this is part of a single secret.

"That I have to be struggle and becoming, goal and clashes between goals: whatever I might create and no matter how much I might love it – soon I will have to oppose it and my love. It is thus that my *will* will have it.

"And even you, you man of enlightenment, are only a pathway and a footstep of my will: my will to power leads the footsteps of your will to truth.

"Only where there is life is there also a will: but not a will to life – rather: will to power!"

Life taught me this once; and I say this to you: everlasting good and evil do not exist! From out of themselves they must overcome themselves – over and over again.

With your values and with your doctrines of good and evil you exercise power, all you evaluators of values. This is your secret love and the shining, trembling, and overflowing of your souls.

But a far greater power and a new overcoming hatch out of your values: both egg and eggshell are smashed against them.

And he who must become a creator in good and evil has to, first, be a destroyer and smash values. [Z]

So far what has advanced humanity the most have been the strongest and most evil spirits: time after time they rekindled passions that were drifting out into a slumber – since ordered society puts the passions to sleep – and they awoke, time after time, the sense of comparison, pleasure in all that is new, audacious, experimental; they forced men to set opinion against opinion, model against model: usually by force of arms, by throwing down boundary markers, by violating all pious sensibilities – but also by inventing new religions and moralities. Thus, in any teacher or preacher of what is *new*, we light upon the same "evil" that makes conquerors infamous, even if its expression is less drastic than this and does not immediately set the muscles in motion, and therefore does not make one quite as infamous. But what is new is *always evil*, being that which desires to defeat and destroy the old boundary markers and the old pious sensibilities – only that which is old is ever good. Good men, in all ages, are those who plough the old thoughts into the earth, planting them deep down and nurturing them until they bear fruit – they are the farmers of the spirit. But eventually all land is exploited, and the ploughshare of evil must return time after time. [GS]

One does not reckon with natures like these; they arrive like fate, without reason, without consideration, without pretext; they arrive as lightning arrives, too terrible, too sudden, too convincing, too "different" to even make it possible to hate them. Their work is an impulsive creation, an imposition of forms; they are the most involuntary, unconscious artists on earth – wherever they appear it is not long before something new emerges, a ruling structure that *lives*, in which parts and functions are delimited and coordinated, in which nothing finds a place that has not first been invested with a "meaning" in relation to the whole. They know nothing of guilt, or responsibility, or consideration, these born organizers; they embody that dreadful egoism of artists that has the look of bronze and knows itself to be justified to eternity in its "work", like a mother in her child. [GM]

These extraordinary promoters of humanity who have hitherto been called philosophers, and who have rarely felt themselves to be friends of knowledge but, on the contrary, to be distasteful fools and dangerous question marks – have found their task, their hard, unwanted, necessary task (and, finally, the great importance of their task) in being the bad conscience of their age. By drawing the vivisector's knife across the *virtues of the age*, they betrayed their innermost secret: to know a new greatness of man, a new unexplored pathway to his transformation. In face of a modern world of "ideas" which struggles to contain everyone in a corner and a "speciality", a philosopher, assuming there could be philosophers in times like these, would labour under a compulsion to see the greatness of man, the whole concept of "greatness", precisely in his spaciousness and in his multiplicity, in his completion in diversity: he would consequently attribute value and rank according to how much of and how many things one could bear to take upon oneself – how *far* one could extend one's responsibility. [BGE]

Everything that has a long life gradually becomes so completely drenched in reason that its irrational origins become improbabilities. Does not almost every accurate history of something leave a ring of paradox and sacrilege against our feelings in our ears? Does not the good historian *contradict* all the time? [D]

Believe me: the secret for reaping the greatest fruitfulness from existence, and the greatest pleasure, is to *live dangerously!* To found your cities on the slopes of Vesuvius! To send your ships sailing out into uncharted seas! To live in a state of war with your peers and with yourselves! To be thieves and plunderers for as long as you cannot be rulers and possessors, you seekers of knowledge! Soon the age will have gone when you could stand any longer to live hidden in the forests like timid deer. At long last the search for knowledge will reach out for its share; it wants to *rule* and to *possess*, and you with it! [GS]

To possess the right to derive value for oneself, to do it with pride, and thus possess the *right to affirm oneself* – this is a ripe fruit, and also a *late* fruit. How long must this fruit have hung upon the tree, unripe and bitter! For an even longer period, nothing at all could be seen of any fruit even vaguely resembling this: no-one could have promised that it would appear, even though everything in the tree was preparing for it – was growing towards it! [GM]

Remain loyal to the earth, my brothers, with all the power of your virtue! Let the overflowing gift of your love and your knowledge confer the meaning of the earth!

Do not let it fly away from the material things of the earth and hammer with its wings against the walls of the Eternal! For there has always been too much virtue that has flown away.

Follow me in drawing flown-away virtue back towards earth – back to the body and to life, so it may bestow upon the earth its meaning: a human meaning.

Spirit and virtue have flown away a hundred times before now and have been botched. Alas, all this illusion and error still lives in our bodies: it has become body and will.

Spirit and virtue have experimented a hundred times before now and have lost their way. Yes, man himself was an experiment. Alas, how much ignorance and error have been embodied in us!

It is not only the reason of millennia, but the madness of millennia which erupts within us. It is dangerous to be an heir.

Step by step along the way, we still fight with the giant called Chance. Until now, mankind has been ruled by the senseless and by the meaningless.

Let your spirit and your virtue serve the meaning of the earth: may the value of all things be reevaluated by you.

From the future arrive breezes stirred by the beating of strong wings. Good news reaches delicate ears.

You solitaries of today shall, in the future, become a people.

From this people shall spring the Overman. The earth shall become a house of healing! [Z]

Nothing like this has ever been written, or felt, or *suffered*: this is how a god suffers, how a Dionysus suffers. The answer to such a dithyramb of solar isolation in the light would be Ariadne. – Who but me knows what Ariadne is! – So far nobody has any solutions for such riddles; I doubt that anyone had noticed that there were any riddles here. [EH]

ARIADNE'S COMPLAINT

Who will warm my heart? Who still loves me?
Hold out your hot hands!
Offer me your heart's coal brazier!
Like a dying man having his feet warmed,
I shake from unknown fevers,
O, how I tremble on the points of icy frost arrows,
Hunted by you, my thought!
Unnameable, veiled one! Dreadful one!
O, hunter behind clouds!
O, mocking eye, flashing out of the darkness!
Struck down by your lightning bolt I lie,
Coiled, twisted, wracked
In every eternal torment,
Struck down
By you, cruel hunter,
Unknowable – God....

Strike deeper!
Strike at me again!
Sting, spike away at my heart –
Puncture it!
What do these punishments hope to achieve

With their toothstump arrows?
Why do you still look down,
Not yet tired of watching human sorrow
With malice flashing in those godlike eyes?
You do not wish to kill,
Only wound, only torture?
But why? Why torture me,
Malicious, unknowable God?
Ha ha!
Why are you creeping up on me
Under cover of midnight?
What do you want?
Speak!
You press upon me, force me down,
Ha! You are far too near!
You hear me breathe,
Listen to my heartbeat,
You jealous eavesdropper!
But jealous for what?
Away! Away!
For what is the ladder?
Would you climb inside my heart?
Would you steal
Into my most secret thoughts?
Shameless, unknown thief!
What do you hope to steal?
What do you hope to overhear?
What torments do you bring,
O, torturer!
O, Hangman-god!
Should I roll in the dirt before you
Like a dog?
Sacrificed, raving with mad passion,
Should I wag in heat for you?
In vain!

Hammer Of The Gods   Friedrich Nietzsche

Stab away,
Cruel thorn!
I am not a dog, but your sport,
Cruellest hunter!
I am the proudest of your prisoners,
Robber behind clouds!
Will you not speak at last?
You, veiled in lightning! Unknowable!
Speak! Highwayman – what do you want from me?

What? A ransom?
What kind of ransom?
Demand much – thus speaks my pride!
And do not haggle – thus speaks my other pride!

Ha ha!
Me – do you want that? Me?
Just me....?

Ha ha!
Then torture me, fool that you are:
Do you presume to injure my pride?
Give me love – who still warms my heart?
Who still loves me?
Hold out your hot hands,
Offer me your heart's coal brazier;
Give me, the most solitary,
Taught by sevenfold layers of ice
To yearn for enemies,
For enemies themselves,
Give me, offer up to me.... yourself,
O, cruellest enemy of all!

He has gone!
He has flown from me,

My only companion,
My best enemy,
My unknown,
My Hangman-god!
No!
Come back to me
With all your torments!
All my tears stream
Along their tracks towards you,
And the last embers of my heart
Burn out for you.
O, come back to me,
My unknowable God! My pain!
My last happiness!

(A flash of lightning. Dionysus appears, shimmering in emerald beauty.)

Dionysus: Be wise, Ariadne, you have small ears, you have my ears: let a wise word slip into them: Must one first not hate oneself, if one is to love oneself? *I am your labyrinth....* [DD]

More than anything else, we are curious to explore the labyrinth. We strive to make friends with Mr. Minotaur, about whom we have been told so many horrific stories. What do they matter to us? – your path which leads upwards, your thread which leads outwards; both of which lead towards you – I am afraid of these.... can you save us all by means of this thread? Above all we beg you, please, straight away, hang yourself on this thread! [PF]

I insist on a final point: among the conditions for a Dionysian life are, in a fundamental way, the hardness of the hammer, the joy even in destruction. The imperative "become hard"! – the basic certainty that *all creators are hard* – is the distinguishing mark of a Dionysian nature. [EH]

I am by far the most fearful human being to have existed; but this does not rule out the possibility that I may be the most beneficial. I know the pleasure of destruction in accordance with my powers to destroy. In both respects, I obey my Dionysian nature which does not know how to separate doing "No" from saying "Yes". I am the first immoralist. This makes me the annihilator *par excellence*. [EH]

I walk among men as one walks among particles of the future – of the future which I seek out.

And all my art and aims strive to bring together and converge into one every particle and riddle and terrible chance.

How could I bear to be a man if this man were not also a poet, a solver of riddles, and the redeemer of chance?

This alone is what I call redemption – to redeem the past and transform every "It was" into "I wanted it to be like this!"

I have taught you that the liberator and bearer of joy is called the will! But also learn this: the will itself remains a prisoner.

To will is to liberate: then what could it be that enchains even the liberator?

"It was": that is what the will's gnashing of teeth, its most lonely affliction, is called. Held powerless against all that which has already been done, the will is an enraged spectator of all that is past.

"That which once was" – that is what the stone it cannot roll away is called.

And because suffering lies within the willer himself, because he cannot will backwards, willing and all life itself is supposed to be a punishment.

No act can be obliterated – how could any act be undone through punishment? That existence itself becomes an eternally returning act and guilt – it is *this* that is what is eternal in that punishment "existence"!

But I lured you away from all these folk songs when I told you: "The will is a creator."

"It was" is a mere particle, a riddle, a terrible chance – until the creative will speaks and says: "But I willed it to be so! And thus shall I will it!" [Z]

One completely botches one's understanding of the beast of prey and the beast of prey in man (for example, Cesare Borgia) when one seeks to discover something "sick" at the core of these most healthy of all tropical monstrosities and growths, or the existence of an innate "Hell" in them: and this is exactly what virtually all moralists have done hitherto. Does it not seem to be the case that within all moralists there lies hatred for the jungle and for the tropics? And the desire to belittle the man of the tropics at any cost, whether this is cast as the sickness and degeneration of man or as his own hell and self-torment? But why? Is it for the benefit of "temperate zones"? For the benefit of temperate men? The moral? The mediocre? [BGE]

In the realm of the stars it can sometimes be two suns that regulate the course of a planet. In certain cases, suns of variable colour shine down on a single planet, first with a red light, then with a green light, and sometimes colliding with it simultaneously, bathing it in multiple shades. The same is true for modern men: we are, thanks to the complex mechanisms of our "starry firmament", regulated by *differing moralities*. Our actions shine in rapidly shifting colours, and they are rarely unequivocal – in many cases, we perform multi-coloured actions. [BGE]

It does not seem strange that lambs dislike great birds of prey: but this gives no ground for upbraiding these birds of prey for making off with little lambs. And if the lambs, among themselves, were to say: "These birds of prey are evil; and consequently, whoever least resembles a bird of prey, and is, rather, its opposite – a lamb – would he not, then, be good?" there would be no reason to criticize this establishment of an ideal, except perhaps that the birds of prey might, among *themselves*, view all this with a certain amount of irony and say: "But we don't dislike these good little lambs in the slightest; actually we love them: nothing is tastier than tender lamb meat!" [GM]

CHAPTER FOUR

WILL TO POWER 2: THE WILL TO THE END

(*All Those Who Love The Age*
The ex-priest and the paroled criminal keep pulling faces: what they desire is a face with no past. – But have you ever noticed those people who realize that their faces reflect the future, and who are so polite to all you people who love the age that they pull a face with no future. [GS])

1. THE LAST WILL OF MANKIND

I tell you this: one must have chaos inside in order to give birth to a dancing star. I tell you: you still have chaos inside you.

But the time is approaching when man will no longer give birth to stars. Alas! The time of the most loathsome man is approaching; the man who is no longer able to despise himself.

Behold! I will show you the Last Man.

The earth has become small, and over its surface hops the Last Man, who makes everything small. His race is ineradicable, like fleas. [Z]

Man has often had enough; there have been actual epidemics of man having had enough (as in c.1348, the time of the dance of death); but still, even this vertigo, this exhaustion, this loathing of himself – all of this is emitted out of him with such explosive violence that it immediately becomes a new fetter. The No he says to life brings to light, as if by some act of magic, an abundance of tender Yeses: even when this master of self-destruction wounds himself, it is the wound that afterwards compels him to *live*. [GM]

It is not fear of man that we should desire to see abated; since this fear is what compels the strong to be strong, and, from time to time, terrible – this fear is what maintains the well-constituted man. What should be feared, what has a more disastrous effect than any other disaster, is that man should cease to inspire profound fear and become the cause of profound nausea. Also – not only great fear, but great pity. If some day these two were to couple, they would inevitably give birth to one of the most uncanny of monsters: the "last will" of mankind, his will to nothingness, nihilism. A great deal already beckons towards this coupling. Whoever is capable of smelling not only with his nose, but also with his eyes and with his ears, almost everywhere picks up something akin to the scent of lunatic asylums and hospitals – I am speaking, of course, of the cultural domain; of every "Europe" on this earth. The *sick* are the greatest threat to mankind; not the evil, not the beasts of prey. All those who are, from the start, failures; the downtrodden, the crushed, the weakest – it is they who must undermine life among men, who call into question and poison our trust in life, in man, in ourselves. Where is it that one does not encounter that veiled glance that weighs one down with deep sadness, that introverted gaze of the born failure which reveals how such a man speaks to himself – the glance which is really a sigh? "If only I were somebody else," it sighs: "but there is no hope of that. I am who I am: how could I ever break free of myself? But still – *I am sick of myself!*" [GM]

They hobble among us like embodied reproaches, as warnings to us – threatening that health, well-constitutedness, strength, dignity, and the feeling of power are, in themselves, vicious things for which one will have to pay one day, and pay dearly: for they are, at bottom, ready to make one pay; they crave to be *hangmen*. Among them hide an abundance of vengeful men disguised as judges, men who wash the word "justice" around their mouths like poisonous spittle, with tightly pursed lips, ever ready to spit upon all those who are not discontented, but mind their own business with good spirits. Neither do they lack among their numbers that most loathsome species of vain, mendacious failures whose sole aim in life is to appear to be "beautiful souls", who peddle their deformed sensuality in the market, swathed in verses and other bandages to look like "purity of heart": the species of moral masturbators and "self-gratifiers". The will to power of the weakest. [GM]

Exhaustion, which wants to reach into the beyond in a single leap, in a death-leap; a wretched, ignorant exhaustion, which no longer wants to want: it is this that created all gods and all afterlives.

It was the body that despaired of the body – it was the body that scratched at the walls of the beyond with the fingers of a deceived spirit. [Z]

2. ANTI-DARWIN

The vaunted "struggle for life" seems to me to have been simply asserted rather than proved. It does occur, but only as an exception: the general economy of life is not hunger and misery, but rather wealth, luxury, even absurd squandering – where the real struggle takes place is in a struggle for power.... One should not mistake Malthus for nature. – If, however, this struggle exists, it results in the reverse of the outcome desired by Darwin's school: the defeat of the stronger, the more privileged, the fortunate exceptions. Species do not evolve into higher perfection: the weak come to dominate the strong again and again – because they are in the great majority, and they are also *cleverer*.... Darwin forgot about the mind (a typically English trait!): *the weak possess more mind*.... To acquire mind one must need mind – one loses it when one no longer needs it. All who possess strength entirely divest themselves of mind. Under the sign of mind I include foresight, patience, dissimulation, rigid self-control, and all mimicry (a large share of all that is virtuous.) [TI]

With the word "Overman" I designate a type of supreme achievement, in opposition to "modern" men, or "good" men; beyond Christians and other nihilists. Almost everywhere, this has been understood, with the utmost innocence, to represent exactly those values which it was set up to destroy – that is as an idealistic vision of a higher type of man, a hybrid of "saint" and "genius".

Some scholarly oafs have even suspected me of Darwinism in this respect. Even "hero worship" of that unconscious and involuntary liar, Thomas Carlyle, which I have maliciously repudiated, has been read onto it. All those to whom I said, in strictest confidence, that it is better to look for a Cesare Borgia in this than a Parsifal did not believe their own ears. [EH]

The Great Advantage Of Polytheism

That an individual may be able to set up his own ideal and by means of it derive for himself his own law, joys, and rights – hitherto this may have been considered to be the most outrageous human provocation possible, and idolatry itself. The few who dared to try this have always felt the need to apologize for themselves, usually by saying: "It wasn't me! Not me! But the work of a god through me!" This great gift, the art of creating gods – polytheism – was the medium through which this impulse could expend, purify, perfect, and enthrone itself; because originally it was a very undistinguished impulse – a product of obstinacy, disobedience, and envy. Opposing this impulse to create one's own ideal was formerly the primary law of all morality. There was only one norm, "man"; and every people thought that it constituted this single norm. But above and outside this, in some distant, higher world, one was permitted to look upon a *plurality of norms* – one god was not considered to be the denial of another god, nor a blasphemy against him. It was in this domain that the luxury of individuals was first permitted. It was here that, for the first time, the rights of individuals were honoured. The invention of all kinds of gods, heroes, and overmen; as well as near-men, half-men, dwarfs, fairies, centaurs, satyrs, demons, and devils, was the preliminary act enabling the justification of egoism and individual sovereignty: the freedom that one granted to a god in his relations with other gods – one finally granted oneself this in relation to laws, customs, and neighbours.

The flip side is monotheism – the rigid consequence of the doctrine of a single, normal human type; the belief in a single, normal god in relation to whom there could only be pseudo-gods – it is perhaps the greatest danger that humanity has ever been faced with. It threatens us with the kind of involution that, as far as we can see, most other species have already reached – for all of them believe in one normal, ideal type for their species, and they have definitively imprinted the morality of mores deep into their own flesh and blood. With polytheism, the pluralism of the free spirit of man reaches its first stage – the power to create for ourselves our own new perspectives – and new perspectives that are, more and more, our own. Man, alone among the animals, has no eternal horizons and perspectives. [GS]

Origin Of The Logical

How did logic come to enter man's head? Certainly by means of illogic, whose domain must, in the past, have been vast. Innumerable entities who made inferences in a way different from ours died out. But, nevertheless, their methods might have been truer. For example: those who did not know how to look for what is "equal" in terms of both nourishment and hostile animals – in other words, those who brought things under concepts too slowly and cautiously – stood less of a chance of survival than those who immediately worked out, in their encounter with similar conditions, that they must be equal. The dominant tendency, namely to treat as equal all that is merely similar – (an illogical tendency, because nothing is equal in any actual sense) – is what created the basis for logic.

In order for the concept of substance to emerge – a concept which is essential for logic, even though nothing real corresponds to it – it was necessary that, for a long time, no-one saw or even perceived the changes in things. These beings who did not have such sensitive perception had an advantage over all those who saw everything "in flux". At base, any degree of caution in making inferences, and every kind of scepticism, pose a threat to life. No-one would have survived if the opposite tendency – to affirm rather than to suspend judgement, to make up errors and fictions rather than to wait, to pass judgement rather than be just – had not been bred in to the point where it became incredibly strong.

The mechanism of logical ideas and inferences in our brain today functions as a process of struggle among impulses: each one of which, taken on its own, is very illogical and unjust. We generally experience only the outcome of this struggle – because this primal mechanism now functions very efficiently, and is well concealed. [GS]

While the noble man lives with himself in trust and honesty, perhaps even with a little naïvety, the man of *ressentiment* is neither upright, nor naive, nor honest, nor straightforward with himself. His soul squints; his spirit loves hiding in holes, secret passages and back doors; everything covert allures him as *his* world, *his* security, *his* nourishment; he knows how to remain silent, how not to forget, how to wait, how to be strategically self-effacing and humble. A race of these men of *ressentiment* is eventually destined to become *cleverer* than any noble race; it will also honour cleverness to a far higher degree: that is, as a condition of existence of primary importance; while among noble men cleverness acquires a delicate flavour of luxury and subtlety – since here it is far less essential than the consummate functioning of the regulating *unconscious* instincts, or even than a certain insolence, a bold recklessness when confronted with danger or with the enemy; or passionate impulsiveness in anger, love, reverence, gratitude, and revenge – the traits by which noble souls have recognized each other at all times. Should it manifest at all in the noble man, *ressentiment* consummates and exhausts itself in an automatic reaction, and therefore does not *poison*. [GM]

Rights Of The Weaker
If one party, say, a besieged city, under certain conditions surrenders to a greater power, the condition it must reciprocate is that this first party can destroy itself, burn down the city, and, in doing this, make the power tolerate a great loss. In this process, a kind of equalization occurs, and, on the basis of

this, rights are established. Preservation is always to the enemy's advantage.

Rights exist between slaves and masters to the same degree, insofar as owning his slave is profitable to the master. At its origin, the *right* exists inasmuch as the one *appears* to be valuable to the other – essential, unchanging, indestructible and so forth. To this extent, the weaker of the two has rights – however modest these might be. Thus the famous maxim "Each has as much right as his power is worth" (Spinoza), or, rather, "as his power is calculated to be." [HH]

The slave revolt in morality begins when *ressentiment* becomes creative and begins to give birth to values: the *ressentiment* of all those natures that are impotent to apply the true reaction to their misery, that of deeds, and compensate themselves with an imaginary revenge. While all noble moralities grow out of a triumphant affirmation of themselves, slave morality, from the start, says No to all that is "outside", all that is "different", all that is not itself; and this No is its creative act. This reversal of the evaluating eye – this *need* to direct the gaze outwards instead of back towards oneself – is the core of *ressentiment*: in order to exist at all, slave morality always needs to seek out a hostile external world; physiologically speaking, it needs external stimuli in order to be able to act at all – its action is fundamentally reaction.

In the noble mode of evaluation, the reverse is the case: it acts and emerges spontaneously, it seeks out its opposite only in order to affirm itself all the more gratefully and triumphantly – its negative concept of "base", "common", "bad", is only invented as an afterthought; a pale, contrasting afterimage in relation to its positive basic concept – brimming with life and passion to the core – "we noble people, we good, beautiful, happy people!" When the noble mode of evaluation sins against and botches reality, it does so in the territory with which it is insufficiently familiar; indeed, against a real knowledge of which it has obstinately guarded itself: in certain circumstances it fails to understand the territory it despises, that of the common man, that of the lower orders. On the other hand, one should recognize that, even presuming the feeling of an affect of contempt, of looking down from a great height, distorts the image of that which is despised, it still remains a far lower magnitude of distortion than that accomplished by its opponent – *in effigy*, naturally – by the substrata of hatred, of vengefulness, in the impotent. There is too much frivolity, too much taking lightly, even too much joyfulness, for it to be able of transforming its object of contempt into a real caricature and a monster. [GM]

3. SUICIDAL NIHILISM

All instincts that do not expend themselves outwardly turn inward. This is what I call the internalization of man. It is by means of this that man first acquired what has come to be known as his "soul". The whole of inner experience, which was originally as thin as it would be if stretched tight between two membranes, expanded. It acquired depth, breadth, and height – to the same extent that outward expenditure was curtailed. All the fearful bulwarks used by the political order to protect itself against the archaic instincts of freedom – punishment among them – turned all these instincts of wild, free, predatory man back *against man himself.* Hatred, cruelty, joy in victimization, pleasure in attacking, in change, in destruction – these were all turned against those who harboured such instincts. That is the origin of the "bad conscience".

The kind of man who, lacking external enemies and obstacles, and imprisoned in the oppressive proximity and conformity of custom, unceasingly flagellated, victimized, chewed away at, attacked, and mistreated himself; the kind of animal that chafed its skin on the bars of its cage ever more as it became domesticated; this poor creature, tormented by a longing to return to the wild, had to turn itself into an adventure, a torture chamber, a strange and perilous wilderness – this fool, this yearning and desperate prisoner, invented the "bad conscience". But here also began the most serious and uncanny kind of sickness, from which humanity has never recovered – man's suffering of man; man's suffering of himself as a disease: the consequence of a forcible severing of ties to his animal past, as if it were a headlong leap into a new environment with new conditions of existence – a declaration of war against the old instincts upon which his strength, joy, and fearful nature had previously rested. [GM]

The first presupposition of this hypothesis concerning the origin of the bad conscience is that the change referred to was neither gradual nor voluntary; it did not take place on account of organic adaptation to new conditions but by a break, a jump, a compulsion, an irresistible catastrophe which immediately ruled-out all possibility for resistance, or even for *ressentiment*. The second is that the fusing of a hitherto unregulated and shapeless population into a solid form was not only constituted by an act of violence – it was also carried to its completion by nothing but acts of violence: that the oldest form of the state appeared as a fearful kind of tyranny, a merciless and oppressive machine which went on working until this raw material of people and half-beasts was not only kneaded and soft, but also *formed*. [GM]

Christianity And Suicide
When Christianity first came into being, there was an immense

thirst for suicide – and Christianity turned this into a lever of its power. Henceforth it permitted only two kinds of suicide, adorned them with the highest dignity and all the highest hopes, and proscribed all others in a terrifying manner. Only martyrdom and the ascetic's slow destruction of his body were allowed. [GS]

What Is The Meaning Of Ascetic Ideals?

In the case of artists they mean nothing at all or far too much; in the case of philosophers and scholars something approaching a sense and instinct for the most auspicious preconditions for a higher spirituality; in the case of women, at best, yet one more seductive charm, a taste of *morbidezza* in luscious flesh, the angelic bearing of a plump, pouting animal; in the case of the physiologically deformed and demented (the *majority* of living beings) an attempt to consider themselves to be "too good" for this world, a saintly form of indulgence, their main weapon in the struggle against protracted pain and boredom; in the case of priests the singular priestly faith, their best instrument of power, also the "supreme" license for power; finally, in the case of saints, an excuse for hibernation, their lust for glory, their slumber in nothingness (i.e. "God"), and their form of insanity. That ascetic ideals have meant so many things to man is an expression of the basic fact of the human will, its horror of the empty void – *it would rather will nothingness than not will at all.* [GM]

In this ideal, the ascetic priest possessed not only his faith but also his will, his power, his interest. His right to exist stands or falls with this ideal: no wonder that, here, we come upon a terrible enemy – supposing ourselves to be enemies of that ideal – we come upon one who fights for his very existence against all who oppose that ideal. [GM]

The idea at stake here is the way in which the ascetic priest evaluates life: he juxtaposes it (and all that belongs with it: "nature", "world", all becoming and transitoriness) with a completely different mode of existence which opposes and proscribes it, unless it turns against itself, unless it denies itself: in that case, the case of the ascetic life, life is a bridge leading to that other mode of existence. The ascetic experiences life as a wrong road, along which one must finally slouch back to the point where it began, or as a mistake to be corrected by deeds – something that *ought* to be corrected: for he *demands* that all should go along with him; where he can, he compels blind acceptance of *his* evaluation of existence. [GM]

Such a monstrous mode of evaluation is branded upon the history of humanity not as an exception or an anomaly, but as one of the most extensive and abiding of all phenomena. Scanned from a distant star, the majuscule script of our terrestrial existence would perhaps result in the conclusion that the earth is a planet of ascetics, a hideout for disappointed, arrogant, and offensive beasts brimming with a deep-set self-loathing, disgust with the earth, disgust with all life; who inflict as much pain upon themselves as they possibly can out of pleasure in inflicting pain. This is probably their sole pleasure. For an ascetic life is a self-contradiction: it is here that *ressentiment* without equal comes to rule, an insatiable instinct and will to power that wants to become master not over something *in* life but over *life itself*, over its deepest, most powerful, and basic conditions – in one case an attempt is made to use force to seal up the wells of force; in another physiological well-being is viewed with disdain, particularly the outward expression of this well-being in beauty and joy; while, on the other hand, pleasure is felt and actively sought-out in sickness, decay, pain, misfortune, ugliness, voluntary deprivation, self- immolation, self-flagellation, self-sacrifice. All this is paradoxical to the highest power: we are confronted with a discord that *wants* to be discordant, that enjoys itself in all this suffering, that even grows more self-confident and triumphant the more its physiological capacity for life atrophies. "Triumph in the ultimate pain": this is the hyperbolic sign under which the ascetic ideal has always gone into battle: in this seductive enigma, in this image of torment and joy, it beheld its brightest light, its salvation, its final victory. [GM]

The thought of men who believe in magic and miracles is determined to *impose a law on nature*; and, in short, religious devotion is the result of this thought. The problem that these men set themselves is clearly intimately linked with this one: how can the *weaker* tribe, in spite of everything, dictate laws to the *stronger*, regulate it, and guide its actions (insofar as they relate to the weaker tribe)? [HH]

Those people who experience their daily lives as empty and monotonous easily become religious: this is understandable and can be overlooked; however, they have no right whatsoever to demand religiosity from those people whose daily lives do not trickle away into emptiness and monotony. [HH]

Why Atheism Today?
"The Father" in God has been completely annulled; as has "the Judge" and "the Rewarder". Also, his "free will": he cannot hear – even if he could hear, he would still not be able to help. The worst thing is this: he seems to be incapable of making himself understood – does this mean he is vague about what he means? – These are all things which, after many conversations, both asking and listening, I was told were the causes of the decline of European theism. It seems to me that the religious instinct is in energetic growth – it merely rejects the theistic solution with profound mistrust. [BGE]

What are the idiosyncrasies of philosophers?.... Their complete lack of a sense of history, their hatred of even the idea of becoming, their Egyptianism. They presume that they honour a thing when they wrench it out of history *sub specie aeterni* (from the viewpoint of eternity), when they mummify it. All that philosophers have dealt in for thousands of years have been conceptual mummies; nothing actual has ever escaped from their clutches alive. They butcher, they stuff, they worship, these conceptual idolaters – when they worship they become a mortal danger to everything. Death, change, aging, as well as reproduction and growth, are objections for them – or even refutations. What is does not become; what becomes is not.... They all believe, to the point of misery, in all that which is. But since they are unable to catch hold of it, they all look for some reason explaining why it is that it is being withheld from them. "It has to be an illusion, a deception which is preventing us from perceiving that which is: where can we find the perpetrator of this deception? – Then they cry out in delight "We've found it! It's the senses! These senses which are so *immoral* are deceiving us about the nature of the *real* world. Moral: escape from the deception of the senses, from becoming, from history, from lies – history is nothing more than belief in the senses, belief in lies. Deny all that trusts in the senses, all the rest of humanity. Be a philosopher, a mummified corpse, represent boring monotheism in a gravedigger vaudeville! – And, above all, deliver us from the body, that contemptible *idée fixé* of the senses! contaminated with every possible error of logic; refuted, impossible, and still impudent to the degree that it insists on behaving as though it actually existed!" [TI]

Delusion Of Idealists
All idealists imagine that the causes they espouse are markedly better than all the other causes in the world. They refuse to believe that if their cause is to flourish at all, it must spring

from the same stinking excremental miasma from which all other human undertakings emerge. [HH]

Fruits And Their Corresponding Seasons
Any better future that one may wish for humanity is also a worse future in some respects, because it would be fanatical to believe that a new, higher state of humanity could unite all the positive traits of earlier stages and would, for example, necessarily produce the highest form of art. Each season has its own value and appeal, and excludes those of other seasons. Whatever has sprung from the roots of religion, and near them, cannot flourish again once religion has been destroyed. Late, stray shoots may well lure us into delusions about it, as may nostalgia for the old art – a condition that may give rise to a feeling of loss and privation, but this is no proof of the existence of any force from which a new art could be born. [HH]

The energies that condition art could die out completely – pleasure in deceit, in confusion, in symbolism, in intoxication, in ecstasy, could all come to be despised. Once the structure of life reaches perfection, then the present time will no longer offer any themes for poetry at all, and only retarded people will still raise demands for poetic unreality. These people would then look back in pangs of nostalgia for the times of imperfection, to the semi-barbarism of our society, our times. [HH]

Whenever the will to power declines in some form there follows a physiological regression, a form of *decadence*. The godhead of *decadence*, stripped of all its manliest drives and virtues necessarily becomes the God of the physiologically disabled, the weak. They, however, do not call themselves the weak; they call themselves the "good".... One will understand at once at what moment in history the double fiction of a good

God and an evil God first became possible. The same instinct which makes the subjugated people reduce its God to the level of the "good in itself" makes them reject the good qualities possessed by the God of their conquerors; they avenge themselves on their masters by transforming their masters' God into a devil. – The good God and the Devil: both are products of *decadence*. – When the preconditions for *ascending* life, when all that is strong, brave, masterful, and proud is eliminated from the concept of God; when, each step of the way, he declines into the symbol of a crutch for the weary, an anchor for all those who are drowning; when he becomes the God of the impoverished, the God of the sinners, the God of the sick, and the predicate "saviour" or "redeemer" hangs in the air as the predicate of divinity as such: what is it that such a transformation attests to? What does such a reduction of the divine speak of? Before he only had his people, his "chosen" people. But in the meantime, just like his people, he has gone wandering abroad; since then he has sat still nowhere, but has been at home everywhere, that great cosmopolitan – to the point where he has got "the great majority" and half the earth on his side. But this democrat among gods has not become a proud, pagan god. He remains the God of the nook, of all dark corners and places, of all the diseased quarters of the world! His is an underworld empire, a hospital, a ghetto.... And he, himself – how pale he has become, how decadent. He was transformed into something which becomes ever paler and less substantial: an ideal, "pure spirit", "absolutum", "thing in itself". The decay of a god. [A]

The Christian conception of God – God as god of the sick, God as spider, God as spirit – is one of the most degenerate conceptions of God ever formulated on earth: it may even represent the lowest tide mark in the retrograde development of the God type. God degenerated into the negation of life, instead of being its transvaluation and eternal affirmation. God is a declaration of war against life, nature, the will to life! God is the formula for every blasphemy uttered against this world in support of the lie of "the next world". In God, nothingness is deified: the will to nothingness becomes sacred! [A]

Christians And Anarchists
When an anarchist, as the very vocal expression of *declining* social strata, self-righteously demands his "rights", or "justice", "equal rights" and the like; he is simply acting under the influence of his lack of culture – which is what prevents him from comprehending *why* it is that he suffers; in *what respect* he is really impoverished – in life.... He is overwhelmed by a cause-creating drive: someone must be to blame for his feeling of self-loathing.... His "righteous indignation" makes him feel good; every poor devil takes pleasure in issuing rebukes – by that he experiences a measure of the intoxication of power. Even howling with complaint can invest life with a charm which makes it worth enduring: every complaint contains a light dose of *revenge*, one blames those who are different for one's own feeling of worthlessness, sometimes for one's actually *being* worthless, as though they were the perpetrators of an injustice, or they possessed an intolerable privilege.... Complaining is useless: it grows out of weakness. Regardless of whether one attributes one's feeling of worthlessness to others or to oneself – the Socialist does the former, the Christian the latter – there is no fundamental difference. What is common to both is that some agent has to be to blame for the fact that one suffers – the sufferer prescribes for himself the honey of revenge as a soothing medication for his suffering. The aims of this thirst for revenge as a thirst for pleasure vary in accordance with circumstances: the sufferer finds opportunities everywhere for cooling-off his petty vengefulness – if he is a Christian, to repeat the point, he finds them in *himself*.... The Christian and the anarchist – both are *decadents*. And when the Christian condemns, abuses, and daubs "the

world" in filth, he does so from the same instinct from which the Socialist worker condemns, abuses, and befouls "society" – the sweet, consoling affect of revenge. [TI]

What? Is the whole of humanity decadent? Has it always been so? What is certain is that it has been *taught* that only decadent values are supreme values. The morality that would strip man of his self is the morality of decline *par excellence* – the fact of the case, "I am in decline," transmuted into the imperative "therefore all of you *ought* to decline." This single kind of morality, all that has ever been taught, the morality of self-denial, reveals a will to the end: it negates life.

The possibility still remains that it is not the whole of humanity which is declining but only that parasitical kind of man – the priest – who has used morality to raise himself to the position of guardian of human values – who finds in Christian morality the means to come to *power*. All the teachers, all the leaders of humanity: all were theologians; but, also, all of them were decadents: hence the transvaluation of all values into hatred of life, hence *morality*. [EH]

Under the influence of the theologian, all value judgements are reversed; the antipathy between "true" and "false" stood on its head: all that which is most life-threatening is here called "true", all that which enriches, intensifies, affirms, or justifies it and enables it to triumph is called "false".... Should it happen that, by way of becoming the "conscience" of princes (or of nations), theologians stretch out their hands for influence, let us be clear about what, at base, is taking place every time this comes to pass: the will to the end, the *nihilistic* will, wants *power*. [A]

Quite separate from the intrinsic value of assertions like "there exists a categorical imperative" is the question: what does an assertion like this tell us about the man who asserts it? Some moralities are set up to justify their authors before others; other moralities are intended to calm him and make him content with himself; using others he seeks to crucify and immolate himself; with others he seeks to exact revenge; with others conceal himself; with others transform himself and enthrone himself on high. Many moralists desire to exercise power and inflict their creative moods on all humanity; whereas others, Kant among them, understand by morality: "What is worthy of respect in me is that I know how to obey – and things *ought* to be no different in your case!" – moralities are no more than a sign language of the emotions. [BGE]

There are many preachers of death: and the earth is full of people to whom departure from life needs to be preached.

The earth is full of superfluous people, the many-too-many, who have compromised life. Let the promise of the afterlife lure them out of this one.

Among them are terrifying creatures who carry a beast of prey chained up inside. They give themselves no choice except lust or self-immolation. Even their lusts are self-immolation.

So far they have not even become men, these dreadful beasts. Let them preach departure from life, and then depart from it themselves!

They are a wasting-disease of the soul: no sooner are they born than they begin to die, and long for comforting doctrines of self-denial and exhaustion.

They would love to be dead, and we should approve of their wish! We must beware of disturbing these dead men from their sleep, of breaking open these living coffins,

Who come upon a cripple, or an old man, or a corpse, and sigh "Life is refuted!"

But it is only *they* who are refuted, they and their eyes that only perceive one face of existence.

Choked in deep depression, and gasping for any accident that may allow death to come, they wait and grind their teeth.

Their wisdom moans: "He who remains alive is a fool; and we are all such fools. That is the most foolish thing in life!"

"Life is nothing but suffering," say others among them, and they do not lie: so make sure that a life which is nothing but suffering ends!

Let the voice of your virtue say: "Kill yourself! Steal yourself away from yourself!"

"Lust is a sin" – say some preachers of death – "let us fall by the wayside and beget no children!"

Others say this – "Giving birth is painful, so why go on giving birth? One only gives birth to unhappy children!" – and they, too, are preachers of death.

"Men ought to be pitied" – say others. "Take from me all that I have! Take all that I am! Because it makes me far less bound to life!"

If they possessed any deep compassion they would strive to make their neighbours loathe life. Evil – that would then be their true good.

But they want to escape from life: what does it matter to them that their chains and gifts bind others more tightly to it?

And you, for whom life is limitless drudgery and unrestrained dread – are you not tired of life? Are you not now ripe for the sermon of death?

All of you for whom frenzied toil, and the swift, the new, and the strange, are precious – you are intolerant of yourselves. Your main preoccupation is flight and the will to completely forget about yourselves.

If you had more belief in life, you would invest less of your attention in the moment. But you are not capable of waiting – nor even of laziness!

The voices of the preachers of death ring out everywhere: and the earth is full of people to whom death needs to be preached –

Or "eternal life": it makes no difference to me – as long as they leave here soon!

Thus spoke Zarathustra. [Z]

CHAPTER FIVE

ON THE ART OF DYING

We would not want to be spared by our best enemies, nor by those who we deeply love.

My brothers in war! I love you from the bottom of my heart; I am, and always have been, one of your number. And I am also your best enemy. So let me tell you the truth!

I know of all the hate and jealousy in your hearts. You are not great enough to know nothing of hate or envy: therefore be great enough to be unashamed of them!

You should be the kind of men whose eyes never stop searching for enemies – for your own enemies; for the ones who you will hate, and who will hate you, at first sight.

You should seek out your enemy, you should fight your war – a war for your opinions. And if your opinion is defeated, your honesty should cry out that it is still a triumph!

You should love peace as a means to waging new wars; and love a short peace more than a long one.

I do not exhort you to go to work, but rather to go to war. I do not exhort you to desire peace, but victory. Your life's work shall be a war; your peace a victory!

One can only rest in silence and peace if one possesses arrows and a bow with which to shoot them – otherwise one only bickers and quarrels.

You say that a good cause raises even war to the sacred? I tell you this: it is a good war that makes every cause sacred.

War and courage have achieved many more great things than has love of one's fellow men. It is not your pity but your bravery that has protected the unfortunate until now.

"What, then, is good?" you ask. It is good to be brave. Leave it to the little girls to bleat "To be good is to be pretty and at the same time moving."

They call you heartless – but your heart is true; I love the modesty of your kind heart. You shame yourself for you flow where others are ashamed of their ebb.

You are ugly? Very well, then, my brothers! Take the sublime around you, wear the mantle of the ugly!

You may have enemies who are worthy of your hate, but none whom you despise. You must be proud of your enemy: then the success of your enemy will also be your success.

Rebellion! That is the mark of slaves! Your emblem is obedience! Let your commanding also be your obeying.

To a noble warrior "You shall" sounds far better than "I will." And everything that you hold dear – you shall let it command you. [Z]

Many die too late and some die too early. But, still, my teaching rings strangely in the ears: "Die at the right time."

To be sure, all those who never lived at the right time could hardly hope to die at the right time. Better for them to wish that they had not been born at all! – I say that to the superfluous.

But even the superfluous accomplish something great with their deaths – even the most hollow nut wants to be cracked.

Death is an important matter for all – but, as yet, death is not a festival. As yet, mankind has not learned to make its most beautiful festival sacred.

I show you the fulfilling death; the death which shall be a spur and a promise to the living.

The man fulfilling his life dies triumphantly, surrounded by hopeful men.

Thus one should learn how to die; and there should be no festival in honour of a dead man who did not know how to consecrate life.

To die thus is the best; but second best is this: to die in battle and squander a great soul.

What the warlike find as hateful as their final conqueror is the grinning death which creeps upon them as a thief – yet also comes as master.

I acclaim my kind of death to you, the voluntary death, which comes because I want it.

But when shall I want it? – Whoever has a goal and an heir wants to die at the time most favourable to his goal and heir.

It is out of deep reverence for his goal and heir that he will seek to hang no more dry funeral wreaths upon the altar of life.

Everyone who wants glory must take leave of honour in good time and practise the difficult art of knowing when to – leave.

Free to die and free in death, one who says No when there is no more time for Yes: he is the one who understands life and death.

That your death may not blaspheme against man and the earth, my friends: I beg this from the honey of your souls.

At the time of your death, your spirit and your virtue should still glow like a long-departed sunset: if not, you will have died a bad death. [Z]

Of all that has been written, I love only that which has been written in blood. Write with blood, and you will soon learn that blood is spirit.

It is not easily possible to understand alien blood: I hate the literate idler.

Whoever writes in blood and aphorisms does not want to be understood: he wants to be learned by heart.

In the mountains, the shortest route passes from summit to

summit – and you must have long legs in order to walk upon it. Aphorisms should be summits, and those to whom they are addressed should be big, tall people.

I want to keep goblins around me, for I have courage. Courage which chases ghosts away creates its own goblins – courage wants to laugh.

I no longer feel the same as you do: I laugh at the black and leaden clouds as they pass beneath me – and these: are they not, precisely, your stormclouds?

You look up into the heavens when you want to be exalted. I look down, because I *am* exalted.

I climb upon the highest mountains, laughing at all tragedies – whether real or imaginary.

Courageous, aloof, mocking, ferocious: thus will our wisdom have us be – for she is a woman and only loves a warrior. [Z]

The great masters of prose have almost always also been poets – if not in public, then at least secretly; behind closed doors. Good prose is written face-to-face with poetry – because it is a continuous, well-mannered war with poetry: all the attractions thereof depend upon the way in which poetry is continually avoided and contradicted. All that is abstract wants to be read as a joke at poetry's expense, with a mocking voice; everything cool and dry is meant to coerce the beautiful goddess into beautiful despair. Often *rapprochements* take place, momentary reconciliations – and then a sudden lunge back and a burst of laughter. Often the curtain is raised and searing light let in just as the goddess is enjoying her dark and muted colours. Often the words are snatched from her mouth and bellowed over a tune that drives her to cover her cultivated ears with her cultivated hands. Thus there are thousands of delights in this war; among them the defeats of which unpoetic souls, the men of prose, know nothing – therefore they write and speak only *bad prose*. "War is the father of all good things" (Heraclitus): war is also the father of good prose. [GS]

I am warlike by nature. One of my instincts is to attack. Being capable of being an enemy, *being* an enemy – perhaps this demands a strong nature: in any case, it belongs to every strong nature. It needs objects to overcome; it searches for what it resists: this aggressive pathos is just as necessarily a component of strength as vengefulness and *ressentiment* is a component of weakness.

The strength of all those who attack can be measured partly by the kind of opposition they seek: all growth is marked by the search for a powerful opponent – or problem; since a warlike philosopher also attacks problems, and faces them in hand-to-hand combat. The task is not just to master all that resists, it is to range all our strength, manoeuvrability, and fighting skill against enemies that are equal to us.

Equality in the face of the enemy is the first requirement for an honest duel. One cannot fight a war against anything that stirs contempt; where one commands, where one can see something beneath oneself, one has no reason to wage war.

My tactics for war can be condensed into four propositions. First: I only attack victorious causes. To this end, I may even wait until they have become victorious.

Second: I only attack causes against which I can find no allies, so that I stand alone against them – so that I can only compromise myself.

Third: I never attack individuals; I simply use the individual as a powerful microscope that allows me to make visible a creeping malady which is general but fundamentally obscured. Thus I attacked Wagner – or, to be precise, the falsity, the loutish instincts, of our "culture"; which misrecognizes subtlety for wealth, and the late for the great.

Fourth: I only attack when there is no question of any personal quarrel; when no backdrop of bad feeling exists. To me, attack is proof of a basic good will – or even gratitude. By associating my name with a cause or person, whether for or against, I honour it. I am entitled to fight against Christianity because I have never suffered misfortunes from this particular quarter. In fact, the most serious Christians have always been well-disposed towards me. I am an enemy of Christianity *de rigueur*, and am not going to blame individuals for the disease of millennia. [EH]

This is war, but war without gunpowder and smoke, without martial posing, without straining limbs: all that would just be idealism. From a torch whose light never falters, a ray of light burns into this underworld of the ideal, where errors upon errors are stacked-up and placed on ice; where the ideal is not refuted – but merely freezes to death. Here, where the "genius" freezes to death; or, around some corner, the "saint"; where the "hero" lies under a huge icicle; and, finally, "faith". "Pity" also cools down; and, everywhere, the "thing in itself" dies from cold. [EH]

Why Do You Write?
A: I am not one of those people who sit thinking while holding an inky pen, and even less one of those people who give themselves over to their passions while sitting on a chair and staring at a piece of paper. My writing annoys me and I am ashamed of it. For me, writing is an urgent and

embarrassing need – and to talk about it, even in the form of a parable, disgusts me.

B: So why do you write? – A: To be quite honest with you, my friend, I have yet to discover any other way of getting rid of my thoughts. – B: But why do you want to get rid of them? – A: Why do I *want* to? Do I want to ? I have to. [GS]

My humanity is a constant process of self-overcoming. [EH]

Why We Are Not Idealists
In the past, philosophers were afraid of the senses. Perhaps it is true that we have forgotten too much of this fear. Today we all believe in the senses, we philosophers of the present and the future, not in theory but in praxis, in practice.

In the past, however, they thought that their senses might entice them away from their own world, the icy realm of "ideas", towards some dangerous island in the south, where they dreaded the thought that their philosophers' virtues might melt down like snow in the heat of the sun. Having blocked ears then was almost a prerequisite of philosophizing; a real philosopher no longer listened to life insofar as life is music; he *refused to hear* the music of life. It is an ancient superstition of philosophers that all music is the music of sirens.

Today we tend to make the opposite judgement (which may turn out to be equally wrong): namely that *ideas* are worse seductresses than our senses ever were, for all their cold and bloodless appearance, and not even in spite of this appearance. They have always preyed upon the "blood" of the philosopher, they have always drained away his senses and consumed his "heart". All these ancient philosophers were heartless; philosophizing itself a form of vampirism. Casting a glance over all these figures, don't you begin to feel something profoundly mysterious and uncanny? Do you not notice the spectacle that rolls out in front of you: how they all become progressively paler? How desensualization is interpreted more and more in terms of the ideal? Do you not sense, concealed in the background, a long-hidden vampire who begins by eating the senses and, in the end, leaves mere bones, mere chatter? By this I mean categories, formulas, *words*; with not a drop of blood left in them. [GS]

In man, both *creature* and *creator* coexist: in man there is matter, fragment, excess, clay, dirt, madness, chaos; but also in man there is creator, sculptor, the hardness of the hammer. *Your* pity is for the "creature in man", for all that needs to be formed, broken, forged, torn, burned, tempered, honed – all that which has to suffer and *should* suffer? As for our pity – do you understand whom our reverse pity is for when it defends itself against your pity as the worst kind of spoiling and weakening? Pity *against* pity, then! [BGE]

Pity is the most enjoyable feeling among people who have very little pride and no prospect of great victories: for them, easy prey – and that is what all those who suffer are for them – is enchanting. Pity is venerated as the virtue of prostitutes. [GS]

The Thought Of Death

Living amid this tangle of little alleys, needs, and voices leaves me in melancholy happiness: how much pleasure, impatience, and desire; how much thirsty life and drunkenness of life is illuminated at every moment. But still, all too soon, silence will envelop these noisy, living, life-thirsty people. Notice how behind everyone lurks his shadow, his dark fellow-traveller. It is always like that final moment before an emigrant's ship casts off: people suddenly have more to say to each other, since the hour is late, and the desolate silence of the ocean looms behind all of this noise – so tightly, and so certainly, does it cling to its prey. And all of them suppose that what has gone before amounts to little or nothing, while the near future is everything; and that is the reason for all of this haste, this confusion, this shouting-down and overreaching each other. Everybody wants to be first to reach into the future – even though death and deathly silence are the only certainties common to all in this future. It is strange that this solitary certainty and common element makes so little impression on people, and that nothing could be further from their minds than the feeling that they constitute a fraternity of death. It makes me happy that men do not want to think the thought of death! What I would very much like to do is something that would make the thought of life merely a hundred times more appealing. [GS]

Measures Against Suicide

There is a kind of justice according to which it is acceptable to take a man's life, but no justice according to which it is acceptable to take his death: this is cruelty, nothing but cruelty. [HH]

Old Men And Death

One may well ask why it is, apart form the dictates of religion, that it is more respectable for a man who is growing old and feeling his powers slip away from him, to sit and wait for his slow exhaustion and decomposition, rather than to put an end to his own life while in complete possession of all his faculties? In this case, suicide is an obvious measure to take, is quite natural, and should inspire great respect for the triumph of reason. Things happened like this in the times when leading Greek philosophers and high-ranking Roman patriots used to die by their own hand. The reverse of all this is far less worthy of respect: the nagging compulsion to stretch life out, day by day, anxiously consulting doctors and being willing to suffer the most painful, humiliating conditions, without the strength to approach the actual goal of life. Religions offer a multitude of excuses for denying the need to kill oneself: this is how they creep into the minds of people who love life. [HH]

The idea of suicide is a powerful comfort: by means of it one survives many a bad night. [BGE]

Death from one's own free choice, death at the right time, taking leave joyfully and with a clear head, death consummated amid children and witnesses so that an actual leave-taking is possible while he who is about to leave is *still there*, in an actual evaluation of all that has been desired and achieved during that life, a summing-up of life – all of this contrasts with the pathetic and horrible comedy that Christianity has made of the hour of death. One should never forget that it has abused the weakness of the dying in order to rape the conscience, and has twisted the mode of death such as to make it possible to make value judgements regarding men and the past! – Here, despite every conceivable cowardice of prejudice, it is above all a question of establishing the correct physiological evaluation of so-called *natural death*: which is, in the end, but one more "unnatural" death – an act of suicide. One dies from no-one but oneself. It is just that "natural" death is death for the most contemptible reasons; an unfree death, death at the *wrong* time, the death of a coward. One ought to desire to die differently if one love's life: to die freely, consciously; not accidentally, not suddenly overtaken.... Finally, a word of advice for the pessimists and all other decadents. We are powerless to prevent ourselves from being born – but this is an error that can be corrected (for it is sometimes an error). When one does away with oneself one does the most admirable thing possible: by it one almost deserves to live! Life derives far more that is advantageous from this than from any kind of "life" wasted in renunciation, green sickness, and virtue – one frees others from having to endure the spectacle of one's objectionable life.... Pure and simple pessimism proves itself only by the self-negation of the pessimist. But, however contagious it might be, pessimism does not add to the general morbidity of an age or race: it is the expression of this morbidity. One succumbs to it just as one succumbs to cholera: one's constitution must already be sufficiently morbid. Pessimism does not of itself produce a single additional decadent: have seen statistics that show that the years in which cholera rages do not differ from any other years in terms of the total number of deaths. [TI]

A man of knowledge must not merely be capable of loving his enemies, but also of hating his friends. One repays one's teacher badly if one remains perpetually a pupil.

You respect me; but what would happen if, one day, your respect were to collapse? Take care, then, that a falling statue does not crush you to death! [Z]

To be incapable of taking one's enemies seriously for very long – or one's accidents, or even one's misdemeanours – *that* is the sign of a strong, full nature in which there is an abundance of the power to form, to mould, to recover, and to forget. Such a man is capable of shaking off, in a single shrug, many of the vermin that bite deep into others. It is here, and here alone, that genuine "love of one's enemies" becomes possible – presuming that it is possible at all on earth. A noble man reveres his enemies – and such reverence is a bridge to love. He desires his enemy for himself, as his mark of distinction; he can bear no enemy but the one in whom there is nothing to loathe and a great deal to honour! The reverse of this is this: "the enemy" as conceived of by the man of *ressentiment* – and here, precisely, is his creation – he produces the "evil enemy", the "Evil One", and this is his basic concept, the one from which he evolves, as an afterthought and pendant to hang around his neck, a "good" man – *himself!* [GM]

The "bad" of noble origin, and the "evil" brewed in the cauldron of accumulated hatred – the former an after-production, a side issue, a contrasting shadow; the latter the reverse: the originary thing, the beginning, the singular act in the birth of slave morality – how different these words "bad" and "evil" are, even though they are both, on the face of it, the reverse of the same concept "good". But it is clearly not the same concept "good": one should ask, rather, exactly *who* it is who is "evil" in the sense employed in a morality of *ressentiment*. The answer is this: the "good" man of the other morality; the noble, powerful man; the ruler, daubed in different, darker colours; interpreted in a different register, seen through the venomous eye of *ressentiment*. [GM]

If anything at all should be held against being sick and being weak it is this – that man's *fighting* instinct wears down. One cannot rid oneself of anything, one cannot recover from anything, one cannot repel anything – everything causes pain. Men and things come in too close; experiences strike one too deeply; memory becomes a festering wound. Sickness is a kind of *ressentiment*.

Faced with all this, the sick person has a single remedy: I call it *Russian fatalism*, the kind of fatalism without revolt exemplified by the Russian soldier who, finding the strain of a campaign too great, lies down in the snow. No longer accepting anything at all, no longer enduring anything, no longer taking anything in – altogether ceasing to react.

This fatalism is not simply something which imbues one with the courage to die; it can also preserve life among the most life-threatening conditions by reducing the speed of the metabolism: a kind of will to hibernation. To push this logic further, we cite the example of the fakir who sleeps for weeks in a grave.

Since one would spend oneself out too quickly if one reacted at all, one no longer reacts: this is the logic. Nothing can burn one out faster than the affect of *ressentiment*. Rage, pathological insecurity, barren thirst for revenge, the concoction of poisons in any way – no reaction could be more perilous for the exhausted: affects such as these involve an accelerated consumption of nervous energy, and a pathological increase of harmful secretions – acid in the stomach. *Ressentiment* is what is forbidden *more than anything* for the sick – it is their singular evil – and, unfortunately, also their most natural inclination. [EH]

A man whose shame possesses depth comes upon his destinies and delicate resolutions along paths which very few people ever reach, and of whose existence his friends and neighbours may not even know: his mortal danger is imperceptible to them, as is the fact that he has regained his sureness of life. A hidden man like this, who automatically uses speech for the purposes of silence and concealment, and is unrestrained in his evasion of communication, *wants* a mask of his face to wander among the heads and hearts of his friends, and he makes certain that it does so – even supposing that he does not want it, he will come to realize that a mask is there anyway, and that it is a good thing. Every profound spirit needs a mask. Further, a mask continually grows around every profound spirit, owing to the continually false, shallow interpretations of every word he utters, every step he takes, every sign of life he shows. [BGE]

What Is Life?
Life – that is: ceaselessly shedding something that desires to die. Life – that is: being cruel and merciless against everything

about us that is becoming old and weak – and not only about *us*. Life – that is, then: being devoid of reverence for all that is dying, all that is wretched, all that is ancient? Constantly being a murderer? But still, old Moses said "Thou shalt not kill." [GS]

THE SUN SINKS

1.

You will not thirst for long,
My burned-out heart!
The promise of something hangs in the air,
In unknown currents which blow upon me –
The great cooling is coming....

My sun burns high up above me at noon:
I welcome you, as you drift by,
You sudden winds,
You cool spirits of evening!

The air surges, strange and clear.
Does the night not
Squint at me with the
Slit eyes of a seducer?
Stand firm, my brave heart!
Do not ask "Why?"

2.

Day of my life!
The sun sinks.
Already the smooth eventide
Is coated in gold.
Warmly breathe the rocks:

Did happiness sleep well at noon –
As it fell into an afternoon slumber?
Now, bathed in green lights,
It plays upon the edge of the brown abyss.

Day of my life!
As you roll towards evening
Your eyes glow pale,
Already half-closed;
Silently,
Your dewy teardrops
Pour into white seas,
Your purple love,
Your last faltering bliss.

3.

Jubilance, golden one, come!
You sweetest and
Most secret foretaste of death!
Have I run my course too fast?
Only now that my feet have tired
Do you catch my eye;
Only now do my fingers grasp your charm.

Around me only waves and games.
Whatever mattered once
Sinks down in blue oblivion –
My boat drifts idle now.
Voyages and storms – how it forgets them all!
Desire and hope have drowned,
Soul and sea are smooth and calm.

Seventh solitude!
Never before have I felt

Your sweet safety closer,
Warmer than sunshine.
Yet does the ice not still glint on my summit?
And now a fish, silver, light,
Swims out of my boat. [DD]

Spirit is the life that strikes at the heart of life: through its own torment it builds up its own knowledge – did you know this?

This is the spirit's joy: to be anointed and consecrated, as a sacrificial animal, by tears – did you know this?

And the sightless gaze of the blind man, and all his seeking and fumbling, shall attest to the power of the sun into which he stared – did you know this?

You have seen only the first sparks of the spirit. You have not seen how the spirit is an anvil, nor have you felt the violence of its hammer!

You have never dared to throw your body down into a pit of snow: you are not yet hot enough to do this! Therefore you have never known the ecstasy of coldness either.

You are not an eagle – so you do not know how the spirit takes joy from terror. And he who is not a bird should not make his nest above the abyss. [Z]

AMONG BIRDS OF PREY

How quickly the deep engulfs
All those who would come down here!
But you, Zarathustra,
Do you still love the abyss,

As do the firs? —

Who strike down roots, where
Even the rocks themselves
Glance down into the depths and shudder –
Who falter on the edge of all abysses
Where everything around
Goes under:
Among the disorder
Of tumbling scree and
Crashing waterfalls, patiently enduring all;
Hard, silent, alone....

Alone!
Who would take the chance
To be a guest down here?
To be your guest?

Maybe only a bird of prey
Who so playfully hangs
He who patiently endures
From his black feathers
With mad laughter; with
The cackle of a predator....

Why so patient?
He contemptuously sneers:
One must have wings, if one loves the abyss....
And should not hang around here
Like you do, hanging man!

O, Zarathustra!
Cruellest Nimrod!
Last stalker of God!
Hunting net of all virtue!

The arrow of the wicked!
Now –
As you hunt yourself down,
Your solitary kill,
It pierces your side....

Now –
Alone with yourself,
In dialogue with what you alone know;
Lost among a hundred mirrors
Returning false likenesses of you;
Among a hundred memories, or more,
Uncertain,
Drained by all your wounds,
Ice-cold in the frost,
Swinging throttled from your own rope,
Self-knower!
Self-hangman!

What have you lashed to yourself
With the noose of your wisdom?
What did you entice into
The paradise of the old snake?
What wormed its way into you?
What burrowed into you?

Only a sick man
Ailing from serpent's venom;
A prisoner
Who suffered the cruellest fate;
Bent double from toil
In your own dark pit;
Holed-up inside
In your own deep grave,
Helpless,

Friedrich Nietzsche   On The Art Of Dying

Stiff,
A cadaver –
Buried under a hundred vices,
Heaped-up upon you,
By you:
The man of knowledge!
The wise Zarathustra!

You sought your most onerous vice:
You found yourself there –
You refused to give yourself up....

Lying,
Crouching,
One who no longer stands up straight;
Crippled spirit, to me
You seem to grow into your grave!

You who so recently stood so tall
Upon all the stilts of your pride!
So recently the godless hermit,
The companion of the Devil,
The scarlet prince of all high spirits!

Now –
Curving between two zeroes,
A question mark;
A tired riddle
For birds of prey....

They have already come to cut you loose,
Yet hunger for your tying together,
They already flutter around you, hanged man!
O, Zarathustra!
Self-knower!

Self-hangman! [DD]

He who knows the heart thoroughly will have realized just
how poor, idiotic, helpless, arrogant, floundering, and more
prone to destruction than redemption is even the best and
deepest kind of love! – It is possible that beneath the holy
facade and fable of the life of Jesus is hidden one of the most
agonizing cases of *knowledge of love*: the martyrdom of the
most innocent and hungry heart, which never had its fill of
human love, which *demanded* love, which demanded solely
to be loved, above all else; which demanded it with severity,
with mania, directing ferocious tantrums against all who denied
it love; the story of an impoverished soul, insatiable in its
craving for love, who had to invent a Hell into which all those
who did not *want* to love it were destined to fall – and which,
having finally become knowledgeable about human love, had
to invent a God who is absolute love, absolute *ability* to love
– who is merciful to human love because it is so very feeble
and ignorant! Whoever harbours feelings such as these,
whoever *knows* about love to this degree – *is seeking death!*
[BGE]

Evil
Scrutinize the lives of the best and most fruitful people and
peoples and then ask whether a tree that is destined to grow
to a proud height can relinquish bad weather and storms;
whether or not misfortune, external resistance, certain kinds of
hatred, jealousy, intransigence, mistrust, hardness, greed, and
violence belong among the favourable conditions without
which any important growth, even of virtue, is impossible. The
poison which destroys weaker natures only strengthens the
strong – nor do they call it poison. [GS]

All animals – including the philosophical animal – strive
instinctively to reach an optimum of favourable conditions

enabling them to expend all their strength and achieve their supreme feeling of power. All animals abhor, every bit as instinctively and with a refined sense of discernment that is "higher than reason", any kind of obstacle that blocks or could block this path to the optimum (and here I do not speak of its path to happiness, but of its path to power, to action, to its most powerful activity – in many cases, then, its path to unhappiness). [GM]

The Ascetic Ideal In The Case Of A Philosopher
He does not deny "existence" as such, but, rather, he affirms *his* existence *alone* – perhaps to the point where he comes close to nurturing the impious wish: *pereat mundus, fiat philosophia, fiat philosophus, fiam!* (Let the world perish, but let there be philosophy, let there be the philosopher, let there be me!). [GM]

When the Christian crusaders in the East came upon the invincible order of the Assassins, that order of free spirits *par excellence*, whose lowest ranks adhered to a rule of obedience the like of which no order of monks ever achieved, they also came upon a clue to the meaning of the symbol and motto reserved for the highest ranks of the sect alone as their *secretum*: "Nothing is true, everything is permitted." – *That* was freedom of spirit; that was the way in which the *faith in truth* was annulled.

Has any European, or any Christian "free spirit" ever wandered into this proposition and all its labyrinthine consequences? Has a single one of them ever encountered the Minotaur that lives in this cave experientially? – I doubt it. I know better: nothing could be more alien to these men, who are unconditional about one thing, than freedom and liberation in this sense – in no way could they be more tightly bound: it is precisely owing to their faith in truth that they are more rigid and unconditional than anyone else. All that constrains these men, this unconditional will to truth, is faith in the ascetic ideal itself, even if it only manifests as an unconscious imperative – it is faith in a *metaphysical* value, the absolute value of truth, secured and guaranteed by this ideal alone – it stands or falls with this ideal. [GM]

Measure is alien to us, let us admit this once and for all; what we itch for is the infinite, the immeasurable. Like riders on charging mounts, we hurtle into the infinite, we modern men, like semi-barbarians. We attain *our* state of rapture only when we are most in danger. [BGE]

LAST WILL

So die,
As I once saw him die –
The friend who cast thunderbolts
And a divine gaze out of my dark youth.
Fearless and deep
In the battle of a dancer

With the brightest stars among warriors,
With the heaviest hearts among victors,
A destiny perched upon his destiny,
Hard, pensive, apprehending –

Shuddering at the thought of victory,
Rejoicing in his triumphal dying,

Sovereign, commanding in death
He commanded that one returns to nothing....

So die,

As I once saw him die:
Triumphant, annihilated. [DD]

From The Military School Of The Spirit
That which does not kill me makes me stronger. [PF]

CHAPTER SIX

WILL TO POWER 3:
THE THIRST FOR REVENGE

Revenge festers in your soul: a black pustule grows wherever you sink in your fangs; your poison makes the soul dizzy with revenge.

It is thus that I speak to you in parables, all you preachers of *equality*, you men who make the soul dizzy! You are tarantulas, and you deal in veiled revenge!

But I will soon lure you out of your hiding places. I tug at your web in the hope that your rage will induce you to leave your cave of lies, and that your revenge will leap forward from behind your word "justice".

That man may be unfettered from the bonds of revenge: that is the bridge leading to my highest hope; a rainbow after a season of storms.

But, of course, the tarantulas would have things be otherwise. They whisper together like this: "That the world shall be lashed by the storms of our revenge – let us call *that* justice.

"We shall exact revenge upon, and do violence to, all those who are not like us." – The hearts of the tarantulas promise themselves this.

"And 'will to equality' – from this moment on we shall mark this with the sign of virtue, and we shall raise an uproar against all that has power!"

These are people of a bad breed and a bad lineage. The hangman and the bloodhound leer out of their faces; and it is precisely they who were once the most vehement world-haters and heretic-burners.

I will not be confused with these preachers of equality, nor do I wish to be taken to be one of their number. Justice speaks *thus* to me: "Men are *not* equal," and nor should they ever become so – what would remain of my love of the Overman if I spoke to you otherwise?

Men should drive towards the future over a thousand bridges and gangways, and there should be more war and more inequality among them!

Good and evil, rich and poor, noble and base, all the names of virtues: these should be used as weapons and resounding symbols, meaning that life must overcome itself over and over again!

My friends, let us also be enemies! Let us divinely struggle *against* each other! [Z]

Two Types Of Revenge

First, let us distinguish the returned blow of retaliation which is almost an involuntary reflex, struck out against even lifeless objects that may have harmed us (such as machines): the purpose of this retaliation is to stop the harm by bringing the machine to a halt. Occasionally, the force expended in the achievement of this aim, the counterblow, is strong enough to smash the machine; and even where it is too sturdy to be destroyed by an individual, he will still strike as hard as he can – making, as it were, an all-out attempt. Against persons who may harm one, one behaves in the same manner; as long as one feels the harm immediately: if you must call this action revenge, then all right; but realize that it is only *self-preservation* that has here set its rational machinery in motion; and that, in the final analysis, one never thought of the person doing the harm in this case, but only of oneself: we may act that way without harbouring any wish to return any harm – we merely wish to escape with life and limb intact.

What is required is *time* when, rather than concentrating on oneself, one begins to concentrate on one's adversary – asking oneself how one can hurt him the most. This is what happens with the second type of revenge: protracted reflection on the other person's weak points and capacity for suffering is its presupposition; one desires to hurt. Protection from further harm is, in this case, such a minor consideration for the seeker of such revenge that he frequently brings further harm down upon himself, and quite often anticipates this in cold blood. With the first type of revenge, it is fear of suffering a second blow which makes the counterstrike as ferocious as possible; but here we come across almost complete indifference to what the adversary *will* do – the strength of the returned blow is conditioned by what he *has* done. But what is it that he has done? Of what use to us could it be if he suffers in the same manner as we have suffered as a result of his actions? What is important here is a *restoration*, while the first type of revenge serves only self-preservation. It may be that, as a result of the adversary's actions, we have lost possessions, status, friends, children; but the restoration is concerned with a sense of loss *incidental* to all these losses. The revenge of restoration offers no protection against further harm; it does not compensate for the harm suffered – except in a single case. If our *honour* has been damaged by our adversary, then revenge may restore it. But this has been damaged in every instance in which suffering has been deliberately inflicted upon us – since our adversary thus demonstrated that he did not *fear* us. Through revenge it is demonstrated that we do not fear him either: this is what constitutes the restoration, the process of equalization.

In the first type of revenge, it is fear that strikes the counterblow; but here it is absence of fear that *desires to prove itself* by hitting back. [WS]

One makes use of dialectics such as these when no other expedient is available. One knows that dialectics inspire mistrust, that they are not entirely convincing. Nothing is easier to counteract than the effect of a dialectician: this is proved by the experience of every speech-making assembly. Dialectics are only ever a desperate last weapon to be used by those who have no other weapons left. One *enforces* one's rights.

As a dialectician, one comes to possess a merciless weapon, with the aid of which one can act as a tyrant; one compromises by conquering. The dialectician leaves it to his adversary to prove that he is not an idiot: he infuriates, and, at the same time, he renders helpless. The dialectician saps the strength of his adversary's intellect. What? is dialectics only a form of *revenge?* [TI]

The kind of faith that primitive Christianity demanded, and

frequently acquired, amid a sceptical and southerly free-spirited world with several hundred years of struggle between philosophical schools behind it, coupled with the education in tolerance provided by the Imperium Romanum – this faith has nothing to do with the rough, true-hearted, citizen's faith which someone like Luther, or Cromwell, or some other northern barbarian of the spirit attached to his God and to his Christianity; it is more like the faith of Pascal, resembling a terrible, drawn-out suicide of reason – a tough, enduring, maggot-like reason which cannot be instantly killed with a single blow. From the start, the Christian faith is sacrifice: sacrifice of all freedom, all pride, all self-confidence; and, at the same time, enslavement, self-mockery, and self-mutilation. there is cruelty and, at the same time, religious Phoenicianism in this faith – drained from an over-ripe, multifarious, and over-indulged conscience: its preconception is that the subjection of the spirit is unspeakably *painful*, that the whole of the past and habitude of this spirit fights against the *absurdity* which "faith" appears to offer it. Modern men, with all their insensitivity to all Christian nomenclature, no longer conceive of the grotesque superlative which, for an ancient taste, lay in the paradoxical idea of "God on the cross". Never before has anyone ever demonstrated comparable boldness in inverting everything; nor anything as fearsome, questioning, and questionable as this ideal: it promised a transvaluation of all antique values. – It is the oriental slave who, in this way, exacted revenge against Rome and its noble, frivolous tolerance: and it has never been faith but *freedom from faith* that has always infuriated slaves about their masters and against their masters. "Enlightenment" infuriates: the slave wants things to be unconditional; in the domain of morality he understands only the tyrannical, he loves as he hates, without sophistication, down into the depths of himself, to the point of pain, to the point of sickness. The great veiled suffering he experiences is infuriated by the noble taste which seems to *deny suffering.* [BGE]

Dante was the perpetrator of a crude blunder when, with awe-inspiring ingenuity, he inscribed these words above the gateway to his Hell: "I too was created by eternal love." Surely there would be more justification for inscribing above the Christian Paradise and its "eternal bliss" the words "I too was created by eternal *hate*" – assuming that a truth can be written above the gateway to a lie! [GM]

The Germans have robbed Europe of the last great cultural harvest it ever reaped – the harvest of the *Renaissance*. Is it yet understood, does anyone yet desire to understand what the Renaissance was? The transvaluation of Christian values; the attempt, using every means, every instinct, every kind of genius, to usher in the victory of the opposing values – noble values.... Before now, this has been the only great war; there has not been a more fundamental interrogation than that undertaken by the Renaissance – the question it raised is the same question that I raise: there has never been a more thoroughgoing attack, nothing more direct, and nothing more forcefully unleashed along the entire frontline, and upon the enemy's centre! To launch an attack on the decisive point, on the very heartland of Christianity, to set noble values on the throne, which is to say feed them into the instincts, the deepest needs and desires of the man who sits on the throne.... I see in my mind's eye an uncannily fascinating possibility – it seems to shimmer with a trembling of refined beauty; there seems to be a diabolically divine art at work in it, something which one might probe the millennia in vain for another instance of: I witness a spectacle simultaneously meaningful and strangely paradoxical, something that would have moved all the gods of Olympus to an immortal roar of laughter – *Cesare Borgia as Pope*.... Am I understood?.... That would have been a victory of the kind I desire today: Christianity would have been abolished! – What went wrong? Luther, a German monk, went to Rome. This monk, with all the resentful instincts of a failed priest squirming inside, howled against the Renaissance in Rome.... Instead of understanding with gratitude the monumental event which had taken place, the overcoming of Christianity in its own seat – his hatred worked out how to nourish itself on this spectacle. All Luther could see was the corruption of the Papacy, even though the reverse was quite obviously the case: the ancient corruption, *the original sin*, Christianity, no longer sat upon the Papal throne! Life sat there instead – the triumph of life, the great Yes to all heightened, beautiful, reckless things!.... And so Luther restored the church: he attacked.... The Renaissance – a meaningless event, great but *in vain!* – O, these Germans, how much they have cost us! In vain – that has always been the main function of the Germans. The Reformation; Leibniz; Kant and so-called German philosophy; the Wars of "Liberation"; *the Reich* – in every instance an in vain for something that already exists, for something *irreversible....* They are my enemies, these Germans, I must say: I loathe about them every kind of impurity of concept and value, all cowardice in the face of an honest Yes and No. For almost a millennium they have distorted and twisted everything that fell into their hands, and they have on their conscience all the half-heartedness from which Europe is sick. They are also responsible for the most degenerate kind of Christianity there is, the most virulent kind, the hardest to refute: Protestantism.... If we never get rid of Christianity, it will be the fault of the Germans. [A]

What have they made of revenge and hatred – these sewer rats dripping with both? Have you heard these words before? Do you not suspect that you are among men of *ressentiment?* ....

"I see nothing, but I hear all the more. I understand. I'll open my ears (O! O! O! and seal my nose against the stench). Now

I can really begin to hear what they have been saying all the time: 'We good men – *we are the just men*' – what they desire they call, not revenge or retaliation, but 'the triumph of justice'; what they hate is not their enemy but 'injustice', what they hate is 'godlessness'; what they believe in and hope for is not the promise of revenge, the euphoria of sweet revenge ('sweeter than honey' according to Homer), but the triumph of God, of the *just* God, over the godless. What remains for them to love on earth are not their brothers in hatred but their 'brothers in love', as they call them, all the good and the just on earth."

– And what do they call the thing which serves to compensate them all for all the misery of life – their phantasmagoria of foretold future bliss?

– "What? Did I hear correctly? They call it 'the Last Judgement', the coming of their kingdom, the coming of the 'Kingdom of God' – in the meantime they live 'in faith', 'in love', 'in hope'!"
[GM]

Throughout the greater part of the course of human history punishment was not inflicted because one held the criminal to be responsible for his criminal act, and thus not on the presupposition that the guilty one alone should be punished: rather, it was meted-out as parents continue to punish their children; from anger at some harm or injury, discharged upon the one who caused it – but this anger is held in control and modified by the notion that every injury possesses an *equivalent* and can actually be paid back, even if only through pain suffered by the perpetrator. And from where did this primeval, deeply rooted, perhaps by now inextirpable, idea draw its power – this idea of an equivalence between crime and pain? From the contractual relationship between *creditor* and *debtor*, which is just as old as the idea of "legal subjects", and which points back towards the elementary forms of buying, selling, barter, trade, and traffic. [GM]

It was here that *promises* were made; here that a memory had to be *made* for those who made promises; here that one encounters a great deal of severity, cruelty, and pain. To inspire confidence in his promise to pay back, to provide a guarantee of the solemnity and sanctity of his promise, to inscribe repayment as a duty, as obligatory for his own conscience, the debtor made a contract with the creditor – and swore that if repayment should not be forthcoming from him, he would substitute something else that he "owned", something over which he exercised control – for example, his body, his wife, his freedom, his life, or, under certain prevailing religious conditions, even his bliss after death, the salvation of his soul, his very rest in the grave (it was just so in Egypt, where even the debtor's carcass found nowhere to hide from the creditor – not even in the grave). But above all, the creditor could inflict every kind of humiliation and torture upon the body of the debtor; for example, hack away from it as much as seemed equivalent to the size of the debt – and everywhere, from ancient times on, there were exact evaluations, *legal* evaluations, of all the individual limbs and body parts with all this in mind, some of which went into horrific and minute detail. [GM]

An equivalence is produced when the creditor receives, in lieu of a literal compensation for an injury (in place of money, land, possessions of any kind), a repayment in the form of a certain kind of *pleasure* – the pleasure of possessing license to discharge his power freely upon one who is powerless, the voluptuous pleasure of "doing evil for the pleasure of doing it", the ecstasy of violation. The lower in the social order that the creditor stands, the greater will his pleasure be – appearing as a delicious morsel, a foretaste of higher rank. In "punishing" the debtor, the creditor participates in a *right of masters*: at long last he, too, may experience the exalted sensation of being allowed to despise and abuse someone "beneath" him – or, at very least, if the actual power and administration of punishment has already passed to the central authorities, to see him despised and abused. Compensation, then, as a license for and a title to cruelty. [GM]

It was here, in the sphere of legal obligations, that the moral world's concepts of "guilt", "conscience", "duty", "sanctity of duty", had their origins. Their origins were, just like the origins of everything that is great on this earth, thoroughly soaked in blood for a long time. Might one not add that this world has never lost a certain fundamental stench of blood and torture? (Not even in dear old Kant: the categorical imperative stinks of cruelty). [GM]

On his way to becoming an "angel" (to avoid using an uglier word) man has developed the nauseous stomach and coated tongue by means of which not only the joy and innocence of the animal repulses him, but also the whole of life itself – to the degree where he sometimes holds his nose in his own presence and, like Pope Innocent III, disgustedly catalogues his own repulsive traits ("....impure begetting, loathsome means of nutrition in the womb of his mother, baseness of the matter out of which man emerges, revolting stench, excretion of saliva, urine, and filth.") [GM]

Against The Defilers Of Nature

I find those people despicable in whom every natural inclination immediately becomes a disease, something that deforms them, or is utterly disreputable: it is they who have seduced us into the belief that man's inclinations and instincts are evil. It is they who have produced our great injustice against our nature, and against all nature. There may well be people who could entrust themselves to their instincts with grace and without care; but they do not, for fear of this imaginary "evil" character of nature. This is why we find so little nobility in men; since it will always be the mark of nobility that one feels no fear before oneself, fears nothing infamous in oneself, we fly out without scruples towards wherever we might feel like flying, like freeborn birds. Wherever *we* go there will always be freedom and sunshine. [GS]

They despise the body: they eliminate it from their reckoning – even worse, they treat it as an enemy. Their most deluded comedy was to believe that one could embody a "beautiful soul" in an abortion of flesh.... In order to make this point believable, it was necessary for them to set up the value of the concept "beautiful soul" to transvalue natural values until, finally, a pale, sick, idiotically gabbling being was set up as perfection – was transfigured into a higher type of man. [PF]

The decadents are the excrement of society – nothing could be unhealthier than taking one's nourishment from these. [PF]

Buying and selling, coupled with their psychological augmentations, are older than the beginnings of any kind of social organization or alliance. It was out of the most rudimentary forms of personal legal rights that the emerging sense of exchange, contract, guilt, rights, obligation, settlement, first transferred itself onto the most vulgar and elementary social complexes (particularly in their relations with other, comparable complexes), together with the custom of comparing, measuring, and evaluating power against power. With the eye keenly focused on this perspective, and with that simple consistency typical of the thinking of primitive humanity, which is difficult to initially mobilize but then proceeds inexorably in the same direction, one arrives at the great standardization: "Everything has its price; all things can be paid for" – the most ancient and most naïve moral measure of *justice*, the beginning of all "good nature", all "fairness", all "objectivity", on earth. Justice at this basic level is the good will between parties of roughly equal power to come to terms with one another; to arrive at an "understanding" by means of a settlement – and to force parties possessing less power to arrive at a settlement among themselves. [GM]

The community, the spurned creditor, will extract whatever repayment it can – one can be certain of this. The direct damage inflicted by the culprit in a crime is of minor significance: the lawbreaker is, above all, a "breaker", a breaker of his contract and his promise to *the whole* with respect to all the benefits and comforts of communal life in which he has hitherto held a share. The lawbreaker is a debtor who has not only failed to make good the benefits and advance payments granted him, but has actually attacked his creditor: therefore he is not just deprived of all these advantages and benefits, as is fair – he is also reminded of *what these benefits are really worth*. The rage of the disappointed creditor, the community, hurls him back into the bestial and outlaw state from which he had hitherto been protected: it throws him away – and now every kind of violence may be inflicted upon him. [GM]

When misfortune strikes, we may overcome it either by removing the cause of it or otherwise by altering the effect it has on our feelings; by which I mean reinterpreting the misfortune as a good, the benefit of which may only become apparent later. Religion, art, and metaphysical philosophy attempt to induce a change in our feelings, in part by altering the way in which we judge experiences, and in part by unleashing a pleasure in pain, or in emotion generally. This is where tragic art has its origins. But the more an individual strives to reinterpret and justify something, the less he will face up to the causes of misfortune and, hence, eliminate them: a fleeting palliation of despair and temporary narcotization (as used in toothache, for example) is enough for him to ride through serious suffering. As the rule of religion and all narcotic arts withers, men confront the thoroughgoing elimination of misfortune more directly. Naturally, this is bad for tragic poets – on account of there now being less and less material for tragedy; because the realm of irreversible, invincible fate is continually diminishing – but it is even worse for priests (because, up until now, they have gorged themselves on the narcotization of human misfortune). [HH]

"I suffer: therefore there must be someone to blame for it" – thinks every sickly sheep. Then his shepherd, the ascetic priest, says: "That is so, my sheep! Someone must, indeed, be to blame for it: you yourself are this someone, you alone are to blame for it – *you alone are to blame for yourself!*" This may be brazen and false enough by itself – but at least it achieves one basic thing: the direction of *ressentiment* is altered. [GM]

For two millennia now we have been condemned to fixing our gaze upon the spectacle of this new type of invalid, "the sinner" – everywhere one may look, one is confronted by the hypnotic stare of the sinner, always fixated on the same object ("guilt" as the single cause of suffering); everywhere the bad conscience, Luther's "abominable beast"; everywhere the past regurgitated, the fact deformed, the "jaundiced eye" for all action; everywhere the will to mistake suffering for the entire content of life, the reinterpretation of suffering as feelings of guilt, fear, and punishment; everywhere the scourge, the hair shirt, the withering body, starvation; everywhere the sinner breaking himself on the wheel of a restless, morbid, lascivious conscience; everywhere muted torment, intense fear, the ecstatic pain of a tortured heart, spasms of an unknown joy, the cry for "redemption". The old depression, heaviness, and weariness were overcome by means of this system of procedures; once more, life became interesting: awake, eternally awake, sleepless, glowing, burned, spent out but not yet exhausted – it was thus that man, "the sinner", was initiated into these mysteries. This powerful ancient sorcerer, the ascetic priest, had obviously won; *his* kingdom had come: one no longer protested against pain, one *thirsted for* pain; "More pain! More pain!" – this is what the desire of his disciples and initiates has howled for centuries. [GM]

Washed-up in the undertow of all this training for repentance and redemption, we come across tremendous epileptic epidemics, the greatest recorded by history, such as the St. Vitus' and St. John's dances of the Middle Ages. As a further after-effect, we encounter hideous paralyses and drawn-out states of depression, which sometimes transform the cheerful temperament of a people or a city (Geneva, Basel) into its reverse side. Here we may also include the passion for witch-hunting; and here we also find those death-seeking mass deliria whose terrible cry of "long live death!" was heard all over Europe, interspersed first with voluptuous idiosyncrasies, then with destructive rages; and the same alternation of these affects, accompanied by the same reversals and gaps between them, will be observed where and whenever the ascetic doctrine of sin achieves an important success. The ascetic ideal and its moral cult, this most ingenious, unscrupulous, and dangerous systematization of all the means of producing orgies of feeling such as these, cloaked in holy intentions, has inscribed itself in a fearful and unforgettable way upon the whole history of humanity – and not only on this history, unfortunately. [GM]

Guilt

Even though the wisest judges of the witches, and even the witches themselves, were convinced of guilt in the crime of sorcery, this guilt nevertheless was an illusion. This applies to all guilt. [GS]

No-one can be held responsible for their actions, no-one for their nature; to judge is to be unjust. This is true to an even greater extent when an individual judges himself. This principle shines as bright as sunlight, but still everyone prefers to skulk in the shadows and in untruth – for fear of the consequences. [HH]

I would prefer to see men remain wild and shameless than through the eyes of their shame and devotion!

Churches they call their sweet-smelling caves!

But who built such caves and prison steps? Who but those people who sought to hide themselves away; who were ashamed beneath the clear sky?

And it will only be when, once more, the clear sky beams through shattered roofs; when, once more, it shines down upon grass and red poppies blooming from broken walls – that I will once again turn my heart towards the places of this God.

All that which negated and harmed them – *that* they called God. To this end, there was great heroism in their worship!

They knew of no way of loving their God other than by hanging men upon the cross!

They strove to live as dead men, they clothed their corpses in black; when they speak I can faintly catch the stench of burial chambers on their breath.

And whoever lives in their vicinity lives in proximity with black pools, out of which the toad, that prophet of evil, croaks its tune with sweet melancholy. [Z]

"My brothers," said the oldest dwarf, "we are in danger. Look at what that giant is about to do: he is on the verge of washing us away with his tears. When a giant cries like a giant it causes a flash flood. If he cries – we're doomed! I don't need to tell you which one of the elements we'll end up drowning in."

"The problem is," said a second dwarf, "how does one prevent a giant from crying like a giant?"

Then, a third dwarf spoke: "The problem is: how does one prevent a great one from doing something great?"

"I'll think about it" – said the oldest dwarf in his dignified manner. "The problem hereby takes on philosophical dimensions; and our interest in it becomes urgent – since we need a quick solution to it."

"We must scare him off!" – said a fourth dwarf.

"We must tickle him!" – said a fifth.

"We must bite his ankles!" – said a sixth.

"Let's do them all at the same time," the oldest decided. "I see that we are equal to this situation in every respect. This giant shall not cry!" [PF]

Flee, my friend, flee into your solitude! I see you deafened by the roar of great men and punctured by the stings of small men.

The forests and the rocks know how to remain silent, like you do. Be like the tree you love, which spreads its branches wide.

It stands swaying over the sea, calm and attentive.

The marketplace begins where solitude ends. Where the marketplace begins, there begins the clamour of all the great actors and the buzzing of poisonous flies.

In this world even the best things are worthless – except for the one who first dramatizes them. The people call these dramatists "great men".

The people have little idea of the greatness which lies in creativity. They only have a taste for all dramatists and actors of great things.

The world revolves around the creator of new values: he is its imperceptible axis. But the people and all glory revolve around actors: this is "the way of the world".

The actor possesses mind, but knows little of the integrity of the spirit. He only believes in the means by which he can produce powerful belief – belief in himself!

Tomorrow he will have a new set of beliefs, and a newer one the day after tomorrow. Like the people, he has a quick wit, and a changeable outlook.

To overthrow – that is, to him, to prove. To inflame with madness – that is, to him, to convince. And spilling blood is the best of all arguments as far as he is concerned.

A truth that slips only into refined ears he calls a lie and a redundant nothing. He only believes in gods who make a roaring noise in the world.

The marketplace is full of solemn clowns – and yet the people still boast of their great men, their idols of the moment!

But they are pressed for time: and so they put pressure on you. They require a Yes or a No from you. Woe to you if you seek to set your chair beyond their For and Against.

Lover of truth, do not be jealous on account of these immovable and oppressive men! Truth has never yet hung from the arm of an immovable man.

Return to where you are safe from these overbearing men. One is only assaulted by Yes? or No? in the marketplace.

The experience of all deep wells is unhurried: they must wait a long time before they realize what has dropped into their depths.

All great things take place away from glory and the marketplace: the inventors of new values have always lived far from these.

Flee, my friend, flee into your solitude: I see you stung by poisonous flies. Flee to where fresh, rough winds blow!

Flee into your solitude! Until now you have lived too close to these small and wretched men. Flee from their veiled revenge! They are nothing but vengeance against you.

Raise your arm against them no longer! They are countless in number, and it is not your destiny to become a fly-swat.

These small and wretched men are innumerable; and many a proud building has been caused to collapse by raindrops and weeds.

You are not made of stone, but, still, these numberless drops have already hollowed you out. You will break apart and burst on account of these many drops.

I see you wearied by poisonous flies, I see you bleed from a hundred punctures; and yet your pride still refuses to be angry.

They want blood from you in all innocence; their anaemic souls crave blood – and so they innocently pierce your side with their stings.

But you are too deep for this, you suffer too deeply – even from small wounds – and before you have had time to recover, the same poisonous worm again crawls all over your hand.

You are too proud to destroy these sweet-toothed insects. But make sure that it does not become your fate to endure all their poisonous injustice.

They buzz around you even when they praise you: and their praise is importunity. They need to get close to your skin and to your blood.

They flatter you as though you were a god or a devil; they whimper before you as they would before a god or a devil. But what of it! They are nothing but flatterers and whimperers.

Often they are kind to you. But that has always been the generosity of cowards. Yes, the cowardly are generous!

They think about you a great deal in their hidebound minds – you always arouse suspicion in them. All that they think about a great deal finally becomes suspicious.

They punish you for your virtues. Fundamentally they will only pardon your mistakes.

Because you are gentle and fair-minded, you say: "They cannot be blamed for their diminutive existence." But their diminutive souls think: "All great existence is blameworthy."

Even when you treat them gently, they still feel that you despise them; and they pay back your kindness with secret cruelty.

Your silent pride always offends them; and if you are ever modest enough to display vanity, they revel in it.

When they recognize a peculiar trait in a man, they always inflate it. So be on your guard against these small men!

They feel themselves to be small beside you; and their lowliness flickers and glows in their secret desire for revenge against you.

Have you not noticed how often they fall silent when you walk among them, and how their strength ebbs away from them like wisps of smoke from a dying fire?

Yes, my friend, you are a bad conscience to your neighbours: because they are not worthy of you. Consequently they hate you, and would dearly love to drink your blood.

Your neighbours will always be poisonous flies. All that is great in you will, itself, make them ever more poisonous and fly-like.

Flee, my friend, flee into your solitude! Flee to where the fresh, rough wind blows! It is not your destiny to become a fly-swat!

Thus spoke Zarathustra. [Z]

CHAPTER SEVEN

THE NEW IDOL

Madness is a rare thing in individuals – but in groups, parties, peoples, ages, it is the rule. [BGE]

Somewhere there are still peoples; somewhere there are still herds – but not here, my brothers. Here there are states.

The state? What is that, then? Open your ears, and I will speak to you about the death of peoples.

The state is the coldest monster of all. It lies coldly; and this is the coldest lie that slithers out of its mouth: "I, the state, am the people."

It is a lie! It was creators who once created peoples and suspended a faith and a love up above them: thus they served life.

It is destroyers who lay traps for the many and call it the state: they suspend a sword and a hundred desires up above them.

The state lies in the language of good and evil. Whatever it says is a lie. Whatever it owns it has stolen.

Everything about it is false. It eats with stolen teeth. Its very innards are false.

I offer you this sign as the sign that marks the state: confusion of the language of good and evil. This sign marks a will to death!

Many-too-many are born, and the state serves these superfluous people!

Notice how it seduces them! How it consumes them, how it chews them up, and then re-chews them! A death for the many that venerates itself as life, a heart-felt service to all preachers of death!

I call the state that place where everyone, be they good or bad, gulps down poison: that place where everyone, be they good or bad, loses themselves: that place where dragging, common suicide is called – life.

These superfluous people! – Notice how they plunder the works of inventors and the prized possessions of the wise. They call this theft their culture, and turn everything into disease and affliction.

These superfluous people! – Notice how they are always sick! They vomit out their bile and call it a newspaper. They consume one another, but are utterly incapable of digesting themselves.

These superfluous people! – Notice how they acquire wealth and yet impoverish themselves. They desire power, and, even more than this, the lever of power – lavish amounts of money.

These nimble apes! – Notice how they scramble over each other, how they tussle their way down into the dirt and the abyss.

They all fight their way towards the throne: this is a mania they all have – as if happiness sat there upon it! But, many times, filth sits perched upon the throne – and the throne itself is perched upon filth.

To me they all seem insane. The idol they worship, that cold monster, smells vile. These idolaters! – all of them smell vile to me.

My brothers, will you stay here and choke in the stench of their animal mouths and animal appetites? It would be better for you to smash the window and spring out into the open air.

Only there, in the place where the state ends, does the man who is not superfluous begin. Only there does the song of the necessary man begin – that singular and irreplaceable melody. [Z]

Parliamentarianism – or, in other words, public license to choose between five or so political opinions – flatters and wins the favour of all those who would like to *appear* to be independent and individual, as if they fought for their opinions. In the end, however, it is a matter of indifference whether the herd is ordered to have one opinion or allowed to have five. Whoever deviates from the five licensed public opinions, and stands apart, will always have the entire herd against them. [GS]

He who is hated by the people as a wolf is hated by the dogs

– it is he who is the free spirit, the enemy of fetters, he who no longer worships, he who lives in the forests.

The people have always called it "having a sense of right" to flush him out of his hiding place: they have always set their most vicious dogs upon him.

"Truth is where the people are! Woe to him who strives for anything else!" It has been like this from the beginning.

And you, all you famous philosophers, you sought to justify the people in their reverence. You called that "will to truth".

But I call him genuine who journeys into godless deserts and breaks his reverent heart.

Burned by the sun upon the yellow sand, he may gaze thirstily at the distant islands filled with springs, on which living creatures rest in the shade of the trees.

But this thirst cannot lure him into becoming like these docile creatures: wherever oases lie, there are also idols. [Z]

Because we have sworn to be faithful, maybe even to a purely chimerical God; because we have bound our heart to a prince, a party, a woman, a religious order, an artist, or a thinker, in the blind mania that engulfed us in rapture and enabled these beings to appear worthy of all honour, all sacrifice: are we, then, inextricably bound? Were we deceiving ourselves? Was it any more than a conditional promise, made under the assumption, the *unspoken assumption*, that those beings to whom we so willingly dedicated ourselves really were the beings we imagined them to be? Must we be faithful to our mistakes even if, by remaining faithful, we damage our higher selves?

No – there is no such law, no such obligation. We need to become traitors, to be unfaithful, to wantonly forsake our ideals again and again. It is not possible to pass from one period of life to another without inflicting these agonies of betrayal, and without suffering from them in turn. Should we then secure ourselves against the irruption of our feeling in order to seal ourselves off from these pains? Would not the world become too bleak, too ghostly, for us to bear? Rather, we should ask ourselves whether this pain inflicted by a change in conviction is *necessary*, or whether or not it depends upon an *erroneous* opinion and evaluation. Why is it that we admire the man who remains faithful to his convictions and despise the one who changes? The answer must be that change in conviction is measured by false standards and that we have, until now at least, suffered too much from these changes. [HH]

Our duties are the rights which others have over us. But how did these others come to acquire these rights? By taking us to be capable of making contracts and repayments, as equal and similar to them; by entrusting us with something on this basis and educating us, correcting us, supporting us. We do our duty – which is to say: we justify this idea of our power on the basis of which we have been treated in this way; we repay according to the same measure as that which has been given to us. We want to regain our sovereignty when we balance what others have done for us by means of what we do for them. [D]

What is actually praised when virtues are sanctified is, first, their instrumental nature and, second, the instinct in every virtue that declines to be held back by any sense of overarching advantage for the individual himself – in sum, the unreason in virtue that leads the individual to permit his transformation into a mere function of the whole. Thus, praise of virtue is praise of something that is privately harmful – the praise of instincts that strip a human being of his most noble selfishness and autonomous strength. [GS]

But let us suppose that what is usually believed to be the "truth" is indeed true – that is that the *meaning of all culture* is the reduction of the beast of prey in man to a docile and civilized animal, *a domestic animal* – then would we not ultimately have to regard all those instincts of reaction and *ressentiment*, which facilitated the overthrow of noble races and their goals, as the *actual instruments of culture?* (Which is not to say that the actual bearers of these instincts themselves actually represent culture). But, on the contrary, is it not that the reverse is probable? – no, further, today it is *palpable!* – these bearers of the oppressive instincts that thirst for revenge, the descendants of every European and non-European slavery, they represent the regression of humanity! These "instruments of culture" are a stain upon man and an accusation and counter-argument levelled against culture in general! One may be quite justified in continuing to fear the beast of prey at the heart of all noble races and in guarding against it: but who would rather not fear a hundredfold, where it is still possible for one to admire, than not fear and be eternally condemned to the repulsive sight of the ill-constituted, shrinking, atrophied, and poisoned? Is this not our fate? And what, today, informs our loathing for "man"?

Certainly not fear, but rather that there is nothing left in man to be afraid of, now that the maggot man swarms and pulses in the foreground; now that the domesticated man, the terminally colourless and pallid man, has taught himself to feel that he is the final goal and the zenith, is the meaning of all history, is the "higher man" – and that he has a certain right to feel like this, insofar as he deludes himself into feeling elevated above the crawling plethora of ill-constituted, sickly, spent-out and exhausted people of which modern Europe is beginning to *stink*. [GM]

To demand of strength that it should not expend itself as strength, that it should not be a desire to overpower, a desire to throw down, a thirst for enemies and struggle and victories, is absurd – the same as demanding that weakness should expend itself as strength. A quantum of power is commensurate to a quantum of drive, of will, of effect – further, it is no more than this driving, willing, and effecting. It is only as a function of the seduction of language (and, hence, of all the inherent errors of reason that are frozen in it), which construes and misconstrues all effects as produced by something that causes effects, by a "subject", that it appears to be otherwise. Just like the mechanism by means of which the popular mind separates the lightning from its flash and takes the latter for an *action*, for the functioning of the subject called lightning; popular morality also separates strength from expressions of strength, as though a neutral substratum stood behind the strong man, which is free to expend its strength or not. But no such substratum exists; there is no "being" behind doing, or effecting, or becoming: "he who acts" is no more than a fiction added to the act – the act is everything. Further, the popular mind doubles the act; when it sees the flash of lightning, it is the act of an act: it posits the same event twice – first as cause, and second as effect. Scientists make no significant improvements when they say "force moves", "force causes", and so on: for all its coolness, for all its lack of emotion, the whole of our science is still governed by the misleading effect of language and has yet to rid itself of that little changeling, "the subject" (for example, the atom is such a changeling; as is the Kantian "thing in itself"). This being given, is it any wonder, then, that the submerged, dark, scowling emotions of vengefulness and hatred mobilize this belief to serve their own ends, and in fact maintain no belief more fervently than this one: that the strong man is free to be weak, that the bird of prey is free to be a lamb? This is how they conferred upon themselves the right to make a bird of prey *accountable* for being a bird of prey. [GM]

"Just" and "unjust" only exist after the institution of the law. To call anything just or unjust in itself makes no sense. *In itself,* no kind of assault, wounding, exploitation, or destruction can be "unjust" – because life itself operates by means of the basic functions of assault, wounding, exploitation, and destruction: and it is not possible to think of them in any way outside this essential character. One needs to assert something even more distasteful; namely that, from the standpoint of biology, legal conditions are only ever exceptional conditions, since they constitute a partial limitation of the will to life, which strives for power, and are subordinated only to its total goal as a single means – a means of producing greater concentrations of power. Any legal order, thought of as sovereign and universal, which functions, not as a means to further struggles between concentrations of power, but as a means of curbing all struggle, will become, in principle, an enemy of life – a germ furthering the dissolution and destruction of man, an attempt to assassinate the future of humanity, a sign of exhaustion, a secret pathway to nothingness. [GM]

The "purpose" of law: this really should be the last thing to mobilize in the history of the origin of the law. For historiography there is no proposition other than the one that it has taken so much time to establish – that really ought to be established now: the cause of the origin of a thing and its eventual use, its actual function and its *place* in a system of purposes, are worlds apart. All that exists, all that has somehow come into being, is repeatedly put to new uses, is repeatedly reinterpreted, captured, transformed, and re-directed by something altogether more powerful than it: all events in the organic world take place in terms of a subduing, a becoming master; and all becoming master requires a new interpretation, a different use of things which obscures, or even destroys, any previous "meaning" or "purpose". No matter how thoroughly one may have understood the utility of any physiological organ (or of a legal system, a social system, a norm of political terminology, a form of art, or a religious cult), one still has not understood its origin: no matter how offensive this may sound to orthodox ears – since it was traditionally believed that if one understood the purpose, the utility of a thing, form, or system, one also understood the reason for its origin – the eye for seeing, the hand for holding....

One formerly imagined that the purpose of punishment was the punishment of criminals. But purposes and utilities are just outward signs that a form of will to power has come to master something less powerful and has imposed upon it a function. The whole history of a "thing", organ, or custom can, in this way, function as a continuous chain of signs which designate new interpretations and forms of capture whose causes do not need to be related to one another but, on the contrary, succeed and reverse each other in a purely aleatory manner. The evolution of a thing, a custom, an organ, therefore has nothing to do with its *progressus* towards a goal, and nothing to with a logical *progressus* using the easiest route available to it by means of the smallest possible expenditure of force. It is a series of more or less profound, more or less mutually independent processes of subduing; the obstacles they come upon, the attempts they make at transformation to the end of defence and reaction, and the results of successful counteractions. Form is fluid – meaning even more so. [GM]

Zones Of Culture
One might say that cultural eras correspond to various climatic zones, with the only difference being that the former follow on from one another, and do not lie next to one another like the

meteorological belts do. Compared with the temperate cultural zone which it is necessary for us to enter, the past gives, for the most part, the lasting impression of a *tropical* climate. Violent divergence; rapid alternation of day and night; fantastic colours and heat; veneration of all things sudden, strange, terrifying; the turbulent onrush of approaching storms; nature's horns of plenty expending themselves wastefully; and, in contrast, our culture; a light, though still not yet brilliant sky; clear, fairly unchanging air; briskness, and sometimes even cold. In this way, the two zones contrast with one another. When we consider how the most violent passions are overcome and dissipated by metaphysical ideas, it sometimes seems like the sight of wild tigers in tropical jungles being strangled in the heavy coils of monstrous snakes. Such things never take place in our spiritual climate – even our fantasies are temperate: even in our nightmares we do not experience what earlier peoples saw while still awake. Now, is it too much to ask that we be happy about this change; granting, for example, that artists are severely hindered by the disappearance of tropical culture, and find those of us who are not artists several shades too sober? In this respect, perhaps artists are correct in denying "progress", because it is certainly open to question whether or not the last three thousand years reveal a course of progress in the arts; in the same way, a metaphysical philosopher like Schopenhauer will have no reason to recognize progress in the course of the last four thousand years of metaphysical philosophy and religion.

But for us, at any rate, the existence of the temperate cultural zone counts as progress. [HH]

Our virtues are conditioned by weakness, *demanded* by weakness.... "Equality", an actual rendering similar of which the theory of "equal rights" is only the expression, belongs to decline: the chasm between man and man, class and class, the multiplicity of types, the will to be oneself, to stand apart – all that which I call the pathos of distance – characterizes every strong age. Today, the tension and the range between extremes is shrinking further and further – the extremes are obliterated to the end point of similarity.... Our political theories and state formations in their entirety are consequences, necessary effects, of decline: the unconscious influence of decadence has gained sovereignty even over the ideals of certain branches of science. My objection to the whole of English and French sociology is that it knows from experience only the decaying forms of society, and innocently presumes that its own decaying instincts are the norm constituting all sociological value judgements. Declining life, the atrophy of all organizing power, i.e. the power to separate, open up chasms and rank above and below, formulates itself in modern sociology as the ideal. [TI]

It may be that there was nothing in the entire prehistory of man more horrifying and uncanny than his *mnemotechnics*: "If something is to be held in the memory it must be branded there: only that which never stops hurting stays in the memory" – this is a proposal of the oldest (and, unfortunately, most enduring) psychology on earth. Man could never live without bloodshed, torture, and sacrifice when he felt the need to create a memory for himself; the most horrific sacrifices and vows (sacrifice of the first-born, for instance), the most repulsive mutilations (castration, for example), the most extremely cruel rites of all religious cults (and all religions are, at base, systems of cruelty) – all this originates from the instinct that realized that pain is the most powerful aid to mnemonics.

In a sense, all of asceticism belongs here: a few basic ideas are to be rendered inextinguishable, enduring, unforgettable, "fixed", to the end of hypnotizing the whole of the nervous and intellectual systems with these "fixed ideas" – and ascetic procedures and modes of life are means by which these ideas are unfettered from competition with all other ideas, in order to make them "unforgettable". The worse man's memory has been, the more dreadful has been the appearance of his customs: the severity of the penal code provides a particularly significant scale against which to measure the magnitude of effort required to overcome forgetting and to impress a series of primitive demands of social existence as *present realities* upon all these slaves to fleeting affect and desire.

For example, consider the old German punishments: stoning (the old sagas have millstones dropping on the heads of the guilty), breaking on the wheel (the archetypal invention and speciality of German genius with regard to punishment!), impaling upon stakes, tearing apart or trampling by horses ("quartering"), boiling in oil or wine, flaying alive, cutting the flesh from the chest, not to mention the practice of smearing the criminal with honey and leaving him out in the burning sun for the flies to devour. Aided by images and procedures such as these, one finally remembers five or six "I will not's" one had promised to obey in order to participate in the benefits of society – and it was also with the aid of this type of memory that one finally came to reason! O, reason, sobriety, mastery over all the affects, that gloomy thing called reflection, all these prerogatives and dramatic routines of man: for what a cost they have all been bought! How much blood and cruelty lie at the base of all "good things". [GM]

In the evening glow of the apocalyptic sun that shone over the Christian peoples, the shadowy figure of the saint loomed to an enormous size; to such a great height that even in these days of ours in which no-one believes in God any more, there are still plenty of thinkers who still believe in saints. [HH]

Until now, nothing has had a more direct power of persuasion than the error of being as formulated by, for the sake of example, the Eleatics: every word, every sentence we utter speaks in its favour! – Even the adversaries of the Eleatics were held subject to the seduction of their own concept of being (Democritus, for example, when he invented his *atom*....). "Reason" in language: O, what a wily old woman! I fear that we are failing to wipe out God because we continue to believe in grammar.... [TI]

EMPOWERMENT THROUGH DEGENERATION

History teaches us that the section of a population that maintains itself best is that part whose members share a vital public spirit, owing to the binding influence of their traditional, irreversible principles – that is, their common faith. The danger inherent to these cemented communities, based on similar, upstanding, individual members, is an escalating, inherited stupidity which follows in the wake of stability as inevitably as a shadow. In communities such as these, intellectual progress depends on those individuals who are less bound, less sure, and morally weaker; men who are prepared to try many new, different things. As a result of their weakness, countless men like these end up being destroyed without registering much tangible impact; but generally, and especially if they have descendants, they unbind things and periodically inflict a wound upon the stable element of the community. It is precisely at this wounded, enfeebled place that the common body is injected with something new. However, the overall strength of the community has to be great enough to take this new element into its bloodstream and assimilate it. Wherever progress is to begin, deviant natures are of premium importance. Every step forward taken by the whole must be preceded by a partial weakening.

Something very much like this takes place in the individual. Degeneration, truncation, or vice, or a loss both physical and moral, rarely take place without being advantageous somewhere else. The sickly man may,finding himself alone for long periods, become more tranquil and wiser; the one-eyed man will possess one eye which sees more vividly; the blind man will possess the faculty of seeing more deeply *inside*, and will certainly hear better.

If a people begins to fall apart and grow weak in one place, but remains strong and healthy in general, it can tolerate being infected by something new, and can incorporate it to its general benefit. When pain and need have come about thus, something new and noble can also inoculate the sites of wounds. [HH]

The Signs Of Corruption
Consider the following signs of such states of society as are necessary from time to time, and which are marked with the term "corruption". Whenever corruption takes hold anywhere, superstition proliferates and the previous common faith of a people pales into impotence against it. Superstition is second-order free spirit: whoever is superstitious is always much more of a person than a religious soul; and a super-stitious society is one in which there are a multitude of individuals and a great pleasure in individuality. Seen in this light, superstition appears as progress, and as evidence that the intellect is becoming more independent as it demands its rights. Those who complain about corruption are followers of the old religion; they are those who have, until this point, determined linguistic usage, and have conferred a bad reputation upon superstition, even among free spirits. Let us be clear that superstition is actually a symptom of enlightenment.

Secondly, any society over which corruption creeps is accused of exhaustion – it becomes obvious that love of war and pleasure in war diminish, while desire for the comforts of life become as intense as desire for military and athletic honours were formerly. What goes generally unnoticed is that the ancient national energy and national passions that became dazzlingly visible in war and warlike games have trickled down into their transmutation into innumerable private passions and have merely become less visible. In times of corruption, the degree of the power and force of the national energies that are expended are greater than ever, as the individual squanders them lavishly – to a degree that he could not have formerly dreamed of when he was not yet rich enough. It is in these times of exhaustion that tragedy runs through houses and through the streets; that burning love and burning hatred are spawned; that the flame of knowledge lights up the sky.

Thirdly, it is often said, as if to compensate for the accusations of superstition and exhaustion, that times of corruption are more gentle – cruelty declines in intensity compared with the earlier, stronger age that was more abandoned to faith. All I am prepared to concede on this point is that cruelty has simply become more refined, and that its older forms become offensive to the new taste. The art of wounding and torturing others with words and looks reaches its paramount development in times of corruption: it is now, and only now, that *malice* and delight in malice are born. The men of corruption are witty and slanderous; they practise types of murder that no longer need daggers or assault – they know that that which is said *well* is believed.

Fourthly, when "morals decline", men emerge whom one refers to as tyrants – they are the forebears and tentative harbingers of *individuals*. In just a short while this fruit of all fruits hangs yellow and ripened from the tree of a people – and the tree only ever existed to bear these fruits. As soon as decay reaches its peak amid the infighting of all kinds of tyrants, a Caesar always appears, the last tyrant, who puts an end to the tired struggle for sole rule by putting exhaustion to work towards his own ends. In this age, the individual is ripest and culture is, therefore, at its most fruitful stage – but neither for his sake nor on account of him, despite the flattery of men of the highest culture who pretend to be the Caesar's creation. In truth, they only need peace from outside because they have turmoil and work enough inside themselves.

In these times, bribery and treason reach their peak, since love of the newly-discovered ego is far more powerful than love of the old, spent-out "fatherland", which has been peddled to death: the need to find some form of security amid the terrifying ups and downs of fortune opens up the noblest hands as soon as anyone who is wealthy and powerful hints that he might be ready to pour gold into them. Hardly anything like a secure future remains; one lives for today, in a state of the soul which makes access to the game easy for all seducers, since one only ever allows oneself to be seduced and bribed "for today", while hanging on to the future and one's virtue.

Individuals care more for the moment than do their opposites, the herd men, because they consider themselves to be no less incalculable than the future itself. They like to fasten themselves to violent men because they endow themselves with a capacity for actions and information that the mass of men would neither comprehend nor indulge, while the tyrant or Caesar understands the rights of the individual even in his wildest excesses, and has a personal interest in advocating a stronger private morality. He thinks of himself, and would have others think of him, in the same way as Napoleon once expressed in his classical manner: "I have the right to answer all charges against me with an eternal 'That's me!' I am apart from the whole world and accept conditions from no-one. I demand subjection even to my fancies, and people should find it quite natural when I give in to this or that distraction." That is how Napoleon once answered his wife when she had reason to question his dubious marital fidelity.

Times of corruption are times when the apples fall from the tree – by which I mean the individuals, the carriers of the seeds of the future, the authors of the spiritual colonization and foundation of new states and communities. Corruption is no more than an unsavoury word for the autumn of a people. [GS]

Socialism is the visionary younger brother of a blind, decrepit despotism whose heir it desires to become. In this respect, its efforts are reactionary in the deepest sense. It desires an abundance of executive power, a wealth of authority comparable only with despotism; indeed, it outstrips anything in the past in its pursuit of the outright destruction of the individual, which it sees as an unjustified luxury of nature, and which it intends to improve by inserting it into the community as an expedient organ. Socialism sprouts up in the immediate vicinity of all excessive displays of power because of its relation to it, just like the typical ancient socialist Plato, at the court of the Sicilian tyrant (Dionysius of Syracuse); it desires to harness, and, in some cases, further the Caesarian state power of this century because, as we said, it desires to become its heir. But even this inheritance would not be enough; it also needs the absolute subjugation of all citizens to the absolute state to a degree that has never before existed. Since it can no longer count on ancient religious piety towards the state, since it has to set itself to work to eliminate piety, *to eliminate all existing states*, it can only hope to maintain itself by means of periodic outbursts of the most extreme terrorism. Therefore, it secretly arms itself for a reign of terror, driving the word "justice" like a nail into the foreheads of the uneducated masses, to rob them completely of their reason, to give them a good conscience for the role in the game they are supposed to play.

Socialism has value only in that it serves, in a brutal and forceful way, to warn of the dangers of all accumulation of state power, and to instill in one a severe mistrust of the state form as such. When its crude voice bellows *"As much state as possible,"* it will at first make this cry noisier than ever; but soon the counter-cry will be heard all the stronger: *"As little state as possible!"* [HH]

GREAT POLITICS

When truth goes into combat with all the lies of millennia, we shall see upheavals, convulsions of earthquakes, a shaking of mountains and valleys, such as has never been dreamed of. The concept of politics will fuse entirely with a war between spirits; all the power structures of the old society will have been blown away – all of them are founded on lies. There will be wars such as have never yet been seen on earth. It is only since I came along that the earth begins to conceive of *great politics.* [EH]

I bring war. Not between people and people: no words are sufficient to express my loathing of the despicable interest-politics pursued by modern European dynasties – politics which make the incitement to self-seeking arrogance among the peoples, setting them against one another, into a principle: and almost into a duty. Not war between classes either – since there are no higher classes, and consequently no inferior ones. What is uppermost in society today is physiologically condemned – so impoverished in its instincts, so unsure of itself, that it actually admits to the possibility of its opposing principle: a higher type of man, a man without scruples.

I bring a war which cuts across all of the absurd coincidences of nation, class, race, status, level of education, constitution – a war like the conflict between rising and falling; between the will to live and the thirst for revenge against life, between upright honesty and treacherous lies.... Because all "higher classes" have been party to these lies, their spirits will never be free, and they must realize this: it is beyond one's capabilities to harbour bad instincts in one's body. Never again, in that case, will it need to be demonstrated just how little the concept of "free will" actually means: one affirms what one is, one negates what one is not.

Great politics will place the physiology of masters above all other considerations; it will forge a power strong enough to create a more complete, higher, type of humanity; while showing merciless severity to all that is degenerate and parasitical upon life – against all that which corrupts, poisons, slanders, judges base, and sees the mark of a higher type of soul in the annihilation of life.

War to the death against vice; every kind of anti-nature is vice, is immoral. The Christian priest is the most immoral type of man, because he teaches anti-nature.

Create a party of life, strong enough for a great politics which will cultivate a higher humanity, which measures the future importance of races, of peoples, of individuals in terms of the magnitude of their inherent relish for life – which will bring an inexorable end to all degenerates and parasites. [PF]

If we could do without wars, so much the better. I can think of many more profitable uses for the twelve billion spent every year to maintain the armed peace in Europe; and other means of gaining respect for physiology preferable to field hospitals. Very well, then: since the old God has been abolished, *I am prepared to rule the world....* [PF]

At this point I am unable to suppress a sigh. There are days when I feel haunted by a sense of blacker than black sadness – the feeling of contempt for man. In order to leave no-one in doubt as to what it is I loathe, who it is that I despise, I tell you: it is the man of today, the man with whom I am fatefully contemporary. The man of today: I choke in the stench of his impure breath.... With regard to the past I am, like all wise men, able to tolerate a great deal – which is to say that I possess a magnanimous kind of self-control: I negotiate the global asylums of entire millennia with a kind of grey vigilance – whether what I am confronted with is called "Christianity", or "Christian faith", or "Christian Church", or whatever, I take care not to hold humanity to be responsible for its crazed nature. But when confronted with the modern age, with our age, my feelings suddenly alter and explode. Our age really *knows....* What used to be merely morbid has become obscene – it is obscene to be a Christian today. My disgust starts from here. I look around: not a single word remains of what used to be known as "truth", we can no longer stand to hear a priest so much as breathe the word. Even possessing only a microscopic claim to integrity one must already know that a theologian, a priest, a pope is not merely mistaken in every sentence he utters – he is always lying, and he is no longer free to lie out of "innocence" or "ignorance".

The priest knows as well as everyone else that there is no "God", no such thing as a "sinner", no "redeemer" – that "free will" and the concept of "moral world order" are lies. Intellectual rigour, the profound self-overcoming of the human intellect, does not allow for the idea that anyone *does not know about these things.* All the concepts of the church are revealed in their true nature: the most malicious set of misnomers possible for the devaluation of nature and natural values. The priest is revealed to be what he has always been: the most dangerous kind of parasite, a venomous spider preying upon life.

Today, we *know*; our conscience knows exactly how much these sinister inventions of priest and church are worth, the end that they serve, the state of human self-violation which is capable of provoking nausea at the sight of humanity – the concepts of "Beyond", "Final Judgement", "immortality of the soul", the "soul" itself: all these are instruments of torture, the expressions of systems of cruelty through which the priest becomes master, and stays master. Everyone knows all this – but, nevertheless, everyone remains unchanged! What has become of the last vestiges of decency and self-respect when even our statesmen, each one of them a practical anti-Christian in all they do, still call themselves Christians and still go to Communion? Or a young prince, riding at the head of his regiments as the highest expression of egoism – professes himself to be a Christian... without any shame! So who is it that Christianity denies? – being a soldier, a judge of one's own law, a patriot, defending oneself, preserving one's honour, desiring to further one's own advantage, to be proud.

The practice of every moment, instinct, or evaluation that leads to action is what is anti-Christian today. Modern man must be a *monster of falsity* to the extent that he remains unashamed of being called a Christian. [A]

– With all this done I pronounce my judgement: I condemn Christianity, I bring against the church the most serious charge that any prosecutor ever uttered. To me it is the most extreme form of corruption it is possible to imagine. The Christian church has left nothing unsoiled by its depravity, it has devalued every value, it has made every truth into a lie, every kind of integrity an indicator of a base soul. And yet people still dare to speak of its "humanitarian" good nature! To abolish states of misery has not been its function: it has lived on states of misery, it has created states of misery, in order to project itself into the eternal.

Take the worm of "sin" for example: it was the church which burdened humanity with this state of misery! – "Equality before God", the lie, the pretext for all the rancour of the weak-minded, the explosive concept which finally became revolution, the modern ideal and the decline of the entire social order – is Christian dynamite....

"Humanitarianism" of Christianity! To harvest a self-contradiction out of humanity, the art of self-violation, a will to falsehood at any cost, to antipathy, to contempt for any honest instinct! These are what Christianity has "blessed" us with. Parasitism as the solitary practice of the church, with its ideal of green sickness, of "holiness" which drains the body of all blood, all love, all confidence in life; the Beyond as the will to deny all reality; the crucifix as the badge of recognition for the most sinister underground conspiracy ever – a conspiracy against life itself.

Wherever there are walls I shall daub this eternal accusation against Christianity, in letters which even the blind can see: I call Christianity the one great curse, the one great expression of depravity, the one great instinct for revenge for which no method could ever be poisonous enough, secret enough, subterranean enough, petty enough – I call it the one immortal disfigurement of humanity.

How is it that one calculates time from the *dies nefastus* (unlucky day) on which this catastrophe arose – from the first day of Christianity? – Why not measure it from its last? From today, then! Transvaluation of all values. [A]

LAW AGAINST CHRISTIANITY [PF]

Given on the Day of Salvation, the first day of Year One (– 30th September 1888 A.D. according to the false calendar).

War to the death against vice: the only vice is Christianity!

First Proposition
Any kind of anti-nature is immoral. The most completely immoral type of man is the Christian priest: he teaches anti-nature. We have no fundamental cause against priests, we merely have prisons for them.

Second Proposition
Any participation in acts in the service of God is an attentat against public morals. Measures taken against Protestants shall be more severe than those taken against Catholics – harder on liberals than on the orthodox. What is criminal about Christianity will gradually be taken up by the masses as they get nearer to the truth about it. Consequently, the philosopher is the worst of all criminals.

Third Proposition
The abominable cities, in which Christianity has incubated and hatched its Basilisk's eggs, will be levelled – razed to the ground and left as fearful monuments to infamy for all time. Poisonous snakes shall be bred in the ruins.

Fourth Proposition
The preaching of chastity is an incitement to public anti-nature. Any kind of scorn for the sexual life, any contamination

of it with the concept of "uncleanliness", is the only real sin against the holy spirit of life.

Fifth Proposition
Anyone who sits down at a table with a priest will be immediately excommunicated from the whole of decent society. The priest is our Chandala – he must be starved-out, ostracized, driven out into the desert, out into every kind of wilderness.

Sixth Proposition
Hagiography, "holy" history, will henceforth be called by the name that it is most worthy of: accursed history. The words "God", "holy man", "redeemer", "saint", will henceforth be used as obscenities – as marks of the lowest kind of criminal.

Seventh Proposition
Everything else follows from this.

—The Anti-Christ

CHAPTER EIGHT

ETERNAL RETURN

Upon The Waterfall
When we look at a waterfall, we may think that we can see free will and choice in the innumerable turnings, meanderings, and breaking of all the waves; but, on the contrary, everything is *necessary*, and it is possible to calculate every movement mathematically. And it is just the same with human actions. If one were omniscient, one would find it simple to calculate every single action in advance, every advancing step on the pathways of knowledge, every error, every act of malice. The acting man is entrapped in his illusion of volition. If the wheel of the world were to stop turning for a second and an all-knowing, calculating mind existed to take advantage of this hiatus, he would be able to plunge deep into the most distant future of all beings, and be able to describe every rut burrowed across the path of the wheel. This self-delusion of the acting man, this assumption that there is such a thing as free will, is also a part of the calculable mechanism. [HH]

Will And Wave

How ravenously this wave comes, as if it were after something!
How it seeps into the most hidden crevices of this labyrinthine
cliff! It seems to be trying to anticipate someone; it seems that
someone of inestimable value must be hiding in there. And
now it washes back, a little more slowly but still foaming white
with agitation – is it disappointed? Has it found what it was
looking for? Is it just feigning disappointment? But already
another wave comes, more ravenous, more savage than the
first – and it, too, seems to be laden with secrets and the urge
to dig for treasures. Thus live waves. And thus live we who
will. I shall say no more about it.

So? You do not trust me? O, beautiful monsters, are you angry
with me? Are you afraid that I will reveal your great secret?
Then be angry with me; arch your menacing green backs up
as high as you can go; build a water-wall between me and the
sun – as you are doing now! Now nothing remains of the
world but a green dusk, slashed across by green lightning.
Carry on as far as you like, bellowing with exuberant joy and
malice – or break once more, pouring out all of your emeralds
into the darkest depths, and flick your infinite white mane of
foam and spray over them. Everything suits me, because
everything suits you so well; and I am grateful to you for
everything – how could I ever think of betraying you? I know
you and your secret, I know your kind! You and I – are we not
the same kind? Do we not share the same secret? [GS]

Parable

All those thinkers for whom the stars move in cyclic orbits are
not the most profound. Whoever looks deep inside himself, as
though into immense space, and carries whole galaxies in
himself, also knows how erratic all galaxies are; they turn
towards the chaos and labyrinth of existence. [GS]

What if some day or night a demon crept after you into your most singular solitude and said: "This life that you now live and have lived, you will have to live it again and countless times again; and there will be nothing new about it; and every pain, every joy, every thought, every sigh, and everything unspeakably great or small in your life will have to return to you, everything in the same progression and sequence – even the spider I see, the moonlight filtered through the trees, even this moment and I myself. The eternal hourglass of existence will be inverted over and over again; as will you, you speck of dust!"

Would you not cast yourself to the ground, grinding your teeth together, cursing the demon who spoke to you thus? Or have you never experienced an immense moment when you would have replied: "You are truly a god, and never before have I been told anything more divine." If this thought possessed you, it would change you where you stood, or maybe it would even crush you. The question "do you desire this to happen once again and countless times more?" would hang upon all your actions as the greatest weight. Or how well disposed towards yourself and towards life would you need to become in order to *crave nothing more* ardently than this ultimate confirmation and seal? [GS]

See this gateway! It has two aspects to it. Here, two paths converge: no-one has ever reached the end of either. The long road behind us stretches out for an eternity. And the long road stretching out before us is also an eternity. These roads stand in opposition to one another; they border one another: and here, at this gateway, they come together. The name of this gateway is written above it: "Now".

But if we were to follow these roads further and ever further on: do you believe that they would oppose each other eternally?

Behold this moment, Now! From this gateway, Now, a long, eternal road stretches backwards: an eternity lies behind us.

Must not all things that *can* run have already run along this road? Must not all things that *can* happen have *already* happened, happened before, and run past?

And if all things have come by here before: what does this make of this Now? Must not this gateway, also, have been here before?

Must it not be that all things are bound inextricably together in such a way that this moment Now draws all future things after it? And therefore draws itself, too?

Because all things that can run must also run ahead, down this long road, yet again.

And this dawdling spider crawling through the moonlight, the moonlight itself, and you and I standing together at this gateway, speaking in muted voices, whispering of eternal things – must it not be that we have all been here before?

And must we not return and run along that other road stretching out ahead of us, along that long, terrible road – must we not recur eternally?

Thus I spoke, my voice growing ever softer: for I was terrified by my own thoughts and reservations. All of a sudden, I heard the howling of a dog close at hand. Had I ever before listened to such howling? My thoughts ran back....

When I was a child I heard a dog howling like that. I saw it, head raised, bristling, shivering in the cold of midnight; the time when even dogs believe in ghosts.

I found myself alone, standing on desolate cliffs, while the most desolate moonlight streamed down.

A man was lying there. And there, the dog; leaping, bristling, whimpering. It saw me coming and howled again – then it *cried out*; it cried out for help.

I had never before seen anything like what I then saw. A shepherd boy lay there writhing, choking, convulsed, his face grotesquely contorted; and a heavy, black snake hung from his mouth.

Had I ever before seen so much disgust and pale horror on a face? Had he, perhaps, been asleep? Then the snake had crawled into his throat and sunk its fangs fast inside.

In vain I tugged and pulled at the snake: my hands could not remove it from the shepherd's throat. From within me a voice cried out: "Bite! Bite!

"Bite its head off!" – cried this voice of all my horror, my hate, my loathing, my pity, my good, and my evil, expelled in a single cry.

All you brave men around me! You explorers, adventurers, and all of you who have set off with cunning sails carrying you over undiscovered seas! All you who take pleasure in riddles!

Solve for me the riddle of what I saw: interpret for me this vision of the most solitary man!

Because it was a vision and a presentiment: *what* did I see in this allegory? *Who* is it that must come one day?

Who is the shepherd, the mouth into which the snake crawled? Who is it that will feel all that is blackest and heaviest thus crawl into his throat?

The shepherd, however, followed the advice I had cried out and bit with a strong bite. He spat out the snake's head, spat it far away from him, and leaped to his feet.

No longer a shepherd, no longer a man – a transformed being, bathed in light – he laughed. Never before had any man laughed as he then laughed!

I heard a laughter that was not human laughter: and now I am consumed by a thirst – a thirst for this laughter overwhelms me – O, how is it that I can bear to go on living? And how could I bear to die after this moment? [Z]

This is your truth: you are too pure to bear the filth of these words: revenge, punishment, reward, retribution.

You love your virtue as a mother loves her child. When did you ever hear a mother demanding payment for her love?

Your virtue is your most highly valued self. The desire of the ring is in you – the ring's desire to attain itself once again – and every ring strives and circles towards that end.

Every achievement of your virtue is like an extinguished star: its light travels eternally – when could it cease to travel? It still travels, even when its work is over. Though forgotten and long dead, its ray of light still shines and travels.

But there are still those in whom virtue squirms under the

whip: you have heeded their cries for far too long!

And there are others who are dragged downwards, sucked under by their devils. But the further down they sink, the more brilliantly shines the longing for God in their eyes.

Still others want to tear the eyes out of their enemies' heads with their virtue. They raise themselves up only in order to lower others.

And there are those who hold it virtuous to say: "Virtue is necessary," but fundamentally believe that only the police are necessary. [Z]

But all joy strives for the eternity of things, it wants honey, it wants crumbs, it wants drunken midnights, graves, the warm consolation of tears at the graveside, golden sunsets. All joy wants itself, and even the agony of its own breaking heart! O, happiness! O, sweet pain! O, breaking heart! All joy wants the eternity of things – *wants deep, deep eternity*. [Z]

For me – how could there be anything outside of me? There is no outside! When we hear music, we forget this; and how sweet it is, this forgetting!

Is it not true that things are given names and sketched in musical notes in order for man to revitalize himself with things?

Sweet, sweet is all speech and all the little falsehoods of music! Through music our love dances on multi-coloured rainbows.

All things dance for those who think as we do. They come to us and offer us their hands, laugh, fly away – and then return.

Everything departs, everything returns; the wheel of existence turns around forever. Everything dies, everything blooms again; the annual cycle of existence rolls on forever.

Everything breaks apart, everything is fixed again; the same house of existence builds itself forever. Everything separates, everything will meet again; the ring of existence is true to itself forever.

The ball that is *There* rolls around everything that we call *Here*. The middle is everywhere. The road of eternity is crooked. [Z]

All things return eternally, and we ourselves with them. We have already existed an infinity of times before, and all things with us.

There is a great year of becoming, a colossal year; and this great year must turn, just like an hourglass, over and over again, until it runs down and runs out over and over again: so that all of these years are alike, both in the greatest and in the smallest things.

"Now I die and rot," you might say, "and in a moment I shall be Nothing. Souls are destined to die as bodies.

"But the complex of causes in which I am enmeshed will recur – it will create me again! I am myself part of all these causes of the eternal return.

"I shall return, under this sun, upon this earth – not to a new life, or to a better life, or to a similar life:

"I shall eternally return to an identical and self-same life, to *this* life, both in the greatest and in the smallest things, to teach again the eternal return of all things." [Z]

Contrary to what the superficial might imagine, forgetting is more than mere inertia; it is an active and in the strictest sense positive mechanism of repression, a mechanism that governs the fact that all we experience and absorb enters our consciousness as little while we are in the process of digesting it as does the thousandfold process of physical nourishment. To shut the doors and close the windows of consciousness for a while; to remain unaffected by the noise and exertion of our underworld of functional organs working both with and against each other; a little peace, a little *tabula rasa* of our consciousness, clearing space for new things; above all for the nobler functions and functionaries – for regulation, foresight, planning (because our organism is an oligarchy) – all this is the purpose of active forgetting, which resembles a doorkeeper, a safeguard of psychic order, calm, and etiquette. It becomes clear that there could be no happiness, no cheerfulness, no hope, no pride, no *present* without forgetting.

But this animal which needs to be forgetful, in which forgetting is an active force, a form of vigourous health, has also bred an opposing faculty in itself, a memory, with the aid of which the action of forgetting is cancelled in certain cases – namely those cases in which promises are made. This involves much more than the passive inability to dispense with an impression, more than mere indigestion from the pledging of a word from which one cannot be extricated, and no less than an active desire not to extricate oneself, a desire for the continuity of something desired once, a real *memory of the will*: with the effect that, between the original "I will," "I will do this," and the actual discharge of the will, its *act*, a world of strange new things and conditions, and even acts of will, may be interposed without breaking this long chain of will. But this presupposes so much! To plan out the future in advance like this, man must first have learned to distinguish necessary events from chance occurrences, to think causally, to see and forecast distant eventualities as though they resided somewhere in the present, to decide with certainty what is the goal and what are the means to it, and be generally able to calculate and compute. Man himself must have become calculable, regular, necessary, even in his self-image, if he is to be capable of deriving value *for his own future*, which is what one who promises does. [GM]

What did the Greeks guarantee themselves in the Dionysian mysteries? *Eternal* life, the eternal return of life; the future promised and consecrated in the past; the victorious Yes to life beyond death and change; *genuine* life as collective continuity through procreation, through the mysteries of sexuality. For this reason the sexual symbol was, for the Greeks, the intrinsic, profound meaning of all piety. Every single detail in the act of procreation, pregnancy, and birth awoke the most exalted and solemn feelings. In the teachings of these mysteries, pain is sacred: the "pains of childbirth" raise pain in general to the level of the sacred – all becoming, all growth, all that endorses the future *postulates* pain.... In order for the eternal joy in creating to exist, for the will to life to eternally affirm itself, the agony of childbirth must also exist eternally.... All this is inscribed in the name Dionysus: there is no higher symbolism than this symbolism of the Dionysian Greeks. The deepest instinct for life, the instinct for the future of life, for the eternity of life, is experienced religiously with this name – the *actual* path to life, procreation, as the *sacred* path.... It was only Christianity, founded upon *ressentiment* against life, which transvalued sexuality into something odious: it daubed filth upon the beginning, upon the precondition of life. [TI]

Affirmation of life, even in its most harsh and most uncanny problems, the will to life celebrating its own inexhaustible nature through the sacrifice of its highest types – *that* is what I call Dionysian. Not so as to purge oneself of pity and terror, not so as to cleanse oneself of a dangerous emotion through its vehement discharge, but, beyond pity and terror, *to realize in oneself* the eternal rapture of becoming – that rapture which also embraces *joy in destruction*.... And with these words I return once more to my point of departure – "The Birth Of Tragedy" was my first transvaluation of all values: with that I once again plant myself in the soil out of which I draw upon all that I will and *can* – I, the last disciple of the philosopher Dionysus, the teacher of the eternal return. [TI]

Onwards
And so travel onwards along the road of wisdom, with a confident gait! Whatever you are, be your own wellspring of experience! Discard all your mistrust in your nature; pardon yourself for your own self, for in it there lies a ladder with a hundred rungs, which you can climb up to knowledge. The age into which you feel you have been cast with sorrow calls you blessed because of this piece of good fortune; it calls to you in order for you to experience things that men in the future will perhaps have to forego.

Do not be ashamed of having once been religious – is it not true that this experience helps you to better understand vast expanses of earlier humanity? Is it not true that many of the best fruits of earlier cultures grew out of that very ground that sometimes displeases you – the ground of impure thought? One must have loved religion like a mother or a wet-nurse – otherwise one cannot be wise to it. And one must also be able to see beyond it, to outgrow it; one understands nothing by remaining enchanted by it.

You must also be familiar with history and be able to play that delicate game with two scales, weighing "on the one hand" against "on the other hand". Stroll backwards, stepping in the tracks through which humanity went on its great and mournful trek through the desert of the past; then you will have surely learned of all the places to where future humanity cannot or may not go back. And by desiring with all your strength to discern in advance how the knot of the future will be tied, your own life takes on the value of a tool and a means, put to the service of knowledge. You have it in your power to merge everything you have lived through – all your experiments, failures, errors, delusions, passions, love, and hope – with your goal, with nothing left empty; you are to become a necessary chain of cultural rings, able to calculate in advance the inevitable course of culture in general. When you can see well enough to make out what lies at the bottom of the dark well of your being and knowing, you may also see it mirror the distant constellations of cultures of the future.

Do you think that a life with such a goal is too hard, too stripped of comfort? Then you still have to learn that no honey tastes sweeter than the honey of knowledge, and that the hanging clouds of sadness above you must serve as an udder, from which you will squeeze milk to nourish yourself. It will only be when you are older that you will understand properly how you listened to the voice of nature, the nature that rules the world by means of pleasure. That life that peaks in old age also peaks in wisdom, in the warm sunshine of continuous joy – you encounter both old age and wisdom on the same plateau of life: and this is how nature meant things to be. Then your time comes – causing no anger as the fog of death comes down. Your final movement – towards the light; your last sound – a joyful cry of knowledge. [HH]

POSTSCRIPT

"THE GENIUS OF THE HEART"

The genius of the heart glowing deep inside that great concealed one, the tempter god and born enticer of consciences, whose voice knows how to plunge down into the underworld of every soul, who says nothing and returns no gaze in which there lies no single trace of seduction, whose mastery resides in knowing how to seem to be – not that which he is but to be what to those who follow his footsteps is one more inducement to press ever closer to him, to follow him ever more inwardly and intensively – the genius of the heart who silences all that is noisy and self-satisfied and teaches it how to listen, who smooths out coarse, rough souls and instills in them a rejuvenated desire to take their time and savour – the desire to stretch out, smooth as a mirror, so that the deep sky may be mirrored in them – the genius of the heart who instructs the rash and impetuous hand to hesitate for a moment and hold onto things more gently; who recovers the hidden and forgotten treasure, the single drop of goodness and sweetness crystallized under thick black ice, and is a divining rod for every little grain of gold which has lain imprisoned in mud and sand; the genius of the heart whose touch enriches all who encounter it, not as though indebted and oppressed by the riches of others, but wealthier in himself, newer to himself than before, cracked open, blown upon and sought out by a thawing wind, maybe less certain, more delicate, fragile, broken apart, but brimming with as yet unnamed hopes, brimming with new will and currents, brimming with new ill will and negative currents.... but what is this that I am doing, my friends? Of whom do I speak? Have I forgotten myself to such a great length that I have neglected to mention his name? Unless you have already realized who this questionable god and spirit is who wants to be worshipped like this. As it happens to everybody who has always been roaming abroad and across foreign territories from his childhood onwards, so has many a strange and not completely harmless spirit strayed across my path – but, above all, over and over again, no less a figure than the great god Dionysus, that great ambiguous tempter god to whom, as you now know, I once offered my first-born in all secrecy and reverence – being, it strikes me, the last person to have tendered him a *sacrifice*: and I have still found no-one who could understand what I was doing in those days. Ever since then I have learned much more, perhaps too much more about the philosophy of this god and, as his last initiate and disciple, perhaps I may be allowed to let you sample some of the flavour of this philosophy, my friends? And in a muted voice – since this will involve a great deal that is secret, new, alien, mysterious, uncanny. The plain fact that Dionysus is revealed to be a philosopher, and that gods therefore philosophize, is a novelty intended to excite suspicion among philosophers – a novelty which is by no means harmless. But it is among you, my friends, that it will be greeted with a warmer reception, unless it should come too late and not at the proper time: for I have come to realize that you no longer believe in God and gods. Maybe now I shall have to make my story more forthright than is perhaps agreeable to the strict habits of your ears? Without a doubt, the aforementioned god went further, much, much further then I in conversations of this type, and I always found myself many steps behind him.... If it was possible to follow that human custom of adorning him in beautiful, solemn titles of grandeur and virtue, above all I would have to venerate his courage as an experimenter and explorer, his fearless honesty, truthfulness, and love of wisdom. But such respectable trash and pageantry rests ill on the shoulders of such a god. He would say: "Keep all that for yourself and your kind, and for anyone else who needs it! I have no reason to shroud my nakedness!" – One will perhaps have noticed that this species of divinity and philosopher is somewhat lacking in shame? – He once spoke thus: "Under certain conditions I love humanity" – gesturing to Ariadne, who was also there – "To me man is an agreeable, ingenious creature with no equal on earth; he knows how to pick his way through every labyrinth. I like him: I often wonder how I may help him to go further and make him stronger, more evil, and deeper than he is at present. Stronger, more evil, more profound, and also more beautiful." And, as he said this, the tempter god smiled his golden smile, as though he had just passed on a charming compliment. [BGE]

Alas, what has finally become of you, my written and painted thoughts? Not so long ago you were still so multi-coloured, so young and vicious, so full of thorns and hidden spices that you made me sneeze and laugh. But now? You have already shed your novelty. I fear that some of you teeter on the brink of becoming truths: already you seem so immortal, so sickeningly righteous, so very boring! Have things ever been different? What is it that we write and paint, we despots with Chinese brushes, we immortalizers of all that allows itself to be written, what are we alone able to paint? Alas, only that which is soon to wither away, all that which is beginning to lose its redolence! Alas, only storms long departed and spent-out; and feelings that have grown old and yellow! Alas, only straggling birds who are ready to drop, exhausted from flight, who allow themselves to fall into our hands! We immortalize all that can no longer live and fly; weary, genial things alone! It is only for your afternoon, all my written and painted thoughts, for which I alone possess the colours in which to express you; many colours, many-coloured loving tendernesses, fiftyfold yellows, browns, greens, and reds. But no-one will be able to tell from all these colours how you once looked – how you looked in your morning, you flashing sparks and marvels of my solitude, my old, beloved, *evil* thoughts! [BGE]

ONLY A FOOL! ONLY A POET!

When the air becomes translucent,
When dew's gentle comfort
Showers down upon the earth,
Invisible, faintly muted –
Since the comforting dew
Puts on dainty shoes like all that softly comforts –
Do you remember, then, my burning heart,
How you once thirsted
For those tears from Heaven, those showers of dew,
Lying scorched, exhausted, thirsting,
When, all the while, on yellow grass trails,
Wicked evening sunbeams
Reached to you through the black treetops –
Blinding, malicious, luminous sunbeams?

"You, the suitor of truth?" they scoffed –
"No! Only a poet!
A crafty, preying, skulking beast
Who has to lie;

Who has to knowingly, wilfully lie,
Lusting for plunder
Behind a coloured mask,
A mask unto itself,
Plunder unto itself –
That – the suitor of truth.... ?
No! Only a fool! Only a poet!
Who speaks colourfully
From behind the coloured masks of fools,
Creeping around on crooked word bridges,
Riding rainbows of lies,
Hovering, crawling prostrate
Beneath a lying Heaven –
Only a fool! Only a poet!

That – the suitor of truth?

Not silent, stiff, smooth, cold,
Become an image,
Become the effigy of a god;
Not erected before temples,
Doorkeeper for a god:
No! The enemy of all such figures of virtue,
More at home in the wilderness than in any temple,
Full of feline malice,
Pouncing through every window,
Spring! Into every chance, go,
Sniffing out every jungle
So you may scramble through the undergrowth,
Sinfully healthy, radiant, colourful,
Among mottled beasts of prey,
Running
With sensuous lips
Blissfully mocking, blissfully hellish,
Blissfully thirsting for blood,

Friedrich Nietzsche   "The Genius Of The Heart"

Preying, creeping, lying....

Or, like an eagle gazing
Into the abyss with a long, long stare,
Staring into its own abyss....
O, how it circles!
Ever deeper under, ever deeper in,
Ever deeper into the depths!
And then,
Suddenly
Diving straight,
Quivering in flight,
It falls upon a lamb,
Plunging down, ravenous,
Thirsting for lambs,
Raging at all lamb-souls,
Fiercely angry with all that looks
Virtuous, sheepish, wool-gathering,
Dull, with a milksop fleece of good will....

Thus
Eagle-like, panther-like
Are the desires of a poet,
Are your desires
Concealed beneath a thousand masks,
You fool! You poet!

You who looked upon humanity
As God and sheep,
To tear apart the God in man,
To tear apart the sheep in man
And, in tearing apart, to laugh –
That, *that* is your rapture;
A panther's and an eagle's rapture,
A poet's and a fool's rapture!"

Hammer Of The Gods   Friedrich Nietzsche

When the air becomes translucent,
When the sickle of the moon,
Green, jealous,
Creeps leaden into the purple twilight,
Enemy of the day,
Scything down hanging gardens of roses
In secret,
Until they sink,
Until they sink down, pale,
Until they sink into the night –
Once I, too, sank thus:
Out of the greenness of my truth,
Out of my daytime yearnings,
Tired of the day, sick of light,
I sank down,
Sank towards evening, towards shadows,
Burned and thirsty
From a single truth –
Do you remember, then, my burning heart,
How you thirsted in those days?

That I am exiled
From all truth!
Only a fool! Only a poet! [DD]

APPENDIX

ARROWS OF MALICE
(BELATED HUMOUR)

1.   Who does woman hate most? Thus spoke the iron to the magnet: "I hate you most of all, because you attract me, but you are not strong enough to pull me to you." [Z]

2.   *The Skin Of The Soul*
Just as bones, meat, intestines, and veins are wrapped in skin, which makes the sight of a man bearable, so the turbulent passions of the soul are covered-up by vanity: it is the skin of the soul. [HH]

3.   *Demolition Of Churches*
There is not enough religion left in the world to make it possible to destroy churches. [HH]

4.   Just as glaciers spread when the sun blazes down on the oceans in equatorial zones with greater heat than before, so a virulent and contagious free-thinking may attest to the fact

---

that, somewhere, emotional heat has greatly intensified. [HH]

5.   *Cyclopses Of Culture*
Confronted with the hollows gouged-out where glaciers have retreated, it is hard to think it possible that a time will come when a valley of pastures, forests, and streams will flourish on the same spot. The same is true for the history of mankind: the most insurgent forces break the way through, coming as destroyers at first; but their activity was necessary, so that a gentler civilization might settle there. The most fearful energies – all that which is called evil – are the cyclopean architects and engineers of humanity. [HH]

6.   Beyond the north, beyond the ice, beyond death: our life! Our happiness! [PF]

7.   We invest no special attention in the possession of a virtue until we notice it lacking in our opponent. [HH]

8.   *Motive For Attack*
We attack a person not only to hurt or conquer them, but also, perhaps, to become aware of our own strength. [HH]

9.   *Most Ugly*
It is doubtful that well-travelled men will have ever seen, anywhere in the world, regions more ugly then those found in a human face. [HH]

10.   *Happiness Of Marriage*
Everything habitual pulls an ever tighter net of spider's webs around us. We notice that the threads have become traps, and that we are sitting in the middle, like a spider who got stuck there and must now feed on its own blood. For this reason, the free spirit hates all habits and rules, and everything enduring and final. That is why, time after time, he painfully tears apart

the mesh enclosing him, even though he will suffer, as a consequence, from innumerable large and small wounds – because he must tear these threads off himself, away from his body, away from his soul. He must learn to hate where he used to love, and vice versa. Nothing is impossible for him, not even the planting of dragons' teeth in the same field in which he used to pour out the cornucopias of his kindness.

Knowing this, one is able to judge for oneself whether one is cut out for the "happiness of marriage". [HH]

11. *Enemies Of Truth*
Convictions are more dangerous enemies of truth than lies. [HH]

12. People who understand something in all its depth rarely remain faithful to it forever. They have brought its depths to light; and there is always a great deal to see in it that is bad. [HH]

13. Throughout the course of history, men have learned that iron necessity is neither iron nor necessary. [HH]

14. Whoever thinks more deeply knows that, whatever his actions and judgements might be, he is always wrong. [HH]

15. Shared joy, not pity, makes a friend. [HH]

16. *The Life Of The Enemy*
Whoever lives for the purpose of fighting an enemy has an interest in their enemy remaining alive. [HH]

17. *The Only Human Right*
He who strays from tradition gets sacrificed to the extraordinary; he who remains bound by it is a slave. Destruction follows in either case. [HH]

18.   *The Way To Equality*

A few hours spent climbing mountains will soon turn a criminal and a saint into two equal creatures. Exhaustion is the shortest way to equality and fraternity. Finally, liberty is added by sleep. [WS]

19.   *Death*

The certainty of death could sweeten all lives with a precious and fragrant drop of light-heartedness. But all you strange pharmacist souls have soured it into a foul-tasting drop of poison which makes the whole of life repulsive. [WS]

20.   We should not allow ourselves to be burned at the stake for our opinions, since we are not that sure of them. But perhaps it would be worth it for this: that we may have and change our opinions. [WS]

21.   I think highly of all scepticism which allows me to reply: "Let's try it." But I do not want to hear anything about things and questions that do not allow experiments. This is the limit of my "sense of truth": courage loses its rights here. [GS]

22.   Wanting to be loved is the highest form of arrogance. [HH]

23.   Love of one is barbaric: because it is practised at the expense of all others. The same goes for love of God. [BGE]

24.   "I have done this," says my memory. "I could not have done this," says my pride – which stands firm until, finally, memory yields. [BGE]

25.   In times of peace the warlike man attacks himself. [BGE]

26.   To find his love requited should really cause the lover

disillusionment with the beloved. "What? She is so modest that she loves even you? Or so stupid? Or.... or...." [BGE]

27.   It is not their love for men but the feebleness of their love for men that stops the Christians today from – burning us. [BGE]

28.   To refuse to hear any more of even the best counter-argument after the decision has been taken is the sign of a strong character – and an occasional will to stupidity. [BGE]

29.   What we do when we dream, we also do while we are awake: we invent and falsify the person with whom we associate – and then, straight away, forget that we have done this. [BGE]

30.   Objection, evasion, humorous suspicion, pleasure in mockery, are signs of health: everything unconditional is pathological. [BGE]

31.   Pity in a man of knowledge is ridiculous – like finding gentle hands on a cyclops. [BGE]

32.   "This is bad! What is he doing? Is he not going – backwards?" – Yes! But how little you understand about him if you witter on about this. He goes backwards in the same way as anyone who is about to make a great jump does. [BGE]

33.   All great human beings radiate retroactive forces: for their sake all of history hangs in the balance, and a thousand secrets of the past crawl out of their holes – to be burned in *their* sunlight. There is no way to tell what may yet become a part of history. Perhaps we still need to discover the past! We still need so many retroactive forces. [GS]

34.   *Horizon Of The Infinite*

We have left the land and departed. Behind us, our bridges
burn – and we have gone even further and burned the land
behind us too. Look out, little ship! Before you is the ocean. It
does not always roar: sometimes it lies smoothed-out like silk
and gold and calm reverie. But there will be times when you
will realize that it is infinite, and that there is nothing more
awe-inspiring than infinity. O, poor bird who once felt free –
how your wings now hammer against the walls of your old
cage! Despair – when you feel homesick for the land, as if it
offered more *freedom*: but there is no longer any "land". [GS]

35.   Mystical explanations for things are considered to be
deep. The fact is that they are not even shallow. [GS]

36.   *Conditions For God*

"God himself cannot exist without clever people," said Luther
– and with good reason. But that "God can exist even less
without stupid people" – that our good Luther did *not* say. [GS]

37.   Holy war has signified the greatest progress of the
masses in the past; because it proves that the mass has begun
to take its concepts seriously. Holy wars only start after the
more refined controversies between sects have refined reason
in general to the point where even the mob becomes subtle,
and begins to take minor points seriously, and actually
harbours the thought that the "eternal salvation of the soul"
might hang on small differences between concepts. [GS]

38.   Thoughts are the shadows of our feelings – always
darker, more empty, and simpler. [GS]

39.   *Kant's Joke*

Kant sought to prove, in a way that would completely confuse
the common people, that the common people were right: that

was his secret joke. He wrote against the scholars in support of popular prejudice, but for scholars and not for the common people. [GS]

40. Anyone with a loud voice is virtually incapable of thinking subtleties. [GS]

41. His whole nature fails to convince us: this is because he will never remain silent about any of his good deeds. [GS]

42. A single miserable person is all it takes to bring cloudy skies of gloom down over a whole household, and it is quite miraculous if there is not one person like that. Happiness is not nearly as contagious. Why? [GS]

43. Even the bravest among us rarely has the courage for what he alone knows. [TI]

44. What? Man is nothing but a mistake of God? Or is it that God is man's mistake? [TI]

45. What? You have chosen virtue and a heaving heart, but, nevertheless, still look upon those who enjoy the advantages of living for today with envy? – But with virtue, one renounces "advantages".... (nailed to the door of an anti-Semite). [TI]

46. Hatred of lies and dissimulation may spring from a sensitive notion of honour. The same hatred may arise out of cowardice, to the extent that lying is forbidden by divine command. Too cowardly to lie.... [TI]

47. *The Disappointed Man Speaks*
I sought great human beings, but all I found were the apes of their God. [TI]

48.   We no longer value ourselves very highly when we communicate. Our inner experiences are not garrulous. They lack words, and would not be able to communicate themselves if they wanted to. We have grown beyond all that we have words for. There is always a grain of contempt concealed in talking. Speech, perhaps, is designed only for the average, the mediocre, the communicable. The speaker vulgarizes himself by speaking. – A moral code for deaf-mutes and other philosophers. [TI]

49.   *The Hammer Speaks*
"Why so hard?" said the charcoal to the diamond; "for are we not closely related?" Why so soft? – I ask you, O my brothers: for are you not – my brothers? Why so soft, pliant, and yielding? Why is there so much denial and self-renunciation in your hearts, and so little fate in your eyes? If you are not fates, if you are not inexorable, then how can you conquer with me? And if your hardness will not flash, and hack to pieces, then how can you create with me? For all creators are hard. And it should seem like ecstasy for you to press your hand down on the millennia as upon wax; ecstasy to engrave upon the millennia as upon metal – harder than metal, more noble than metal. The most noble thing is perfectly hard. I suspend this new law-tablet above you, O my brothers: become hard! [Z & TI]

50.   At best, in one's wild nature, one recovers from one's anti-nature – from "spirituality".... [PF]

51.   Murder and suicide belong together and follow each other in proportion to age and the time of year. Pessimism and suicide belong together.... [PF]

52.   Woman, the "Eternal Feminine": nothing but an imaginary value, which man is alone in believing in. [PF]

53.   Whoever laughs best also laughs last. [PF]

54.   Great style follows in the wake of great passion. It disdains to please, it neglects to argue. It commands. It will. [PF]

55.   Man is a mediocre egoist: even the wisest man takes convention to be more important than his own interests. [PF]

56.   Sickness is a powerful stimulant. Now all one needs is the strength to swallow it. [PF]

57.   "You still do not know what you need in order to multiply your power by ten?" – What? Hangers-on? – "No. Zeroes!" [PF]

58.   The whole of our sociology knows of no other instinct than that of the herd, that is: the sum of zero – where every zero has "equal rights", where it is virtuous to be zero. [PF]

59.   Something Muhammedanism has learned from the Christians: the use of "the Beyond" as a punishment organ. [PF]

AMONG THE DAUGHTERS OF THE DESERT

Deserts grow: woe to him who harbours deserts!

Ahem! Formally!
Yes, formally –
A good way to begin,
In a solemn, African way,
Worthy of a lion,
Or the moral jabbering of an ape!
– But it means nothing to you,
You dearest maidens,

At whose feet I,
A European beneath the palm trees,
Am allowed to sit,
For the first time. Selah.

Truly wonderful!
Here I sit,
With the desert before me,
And yet so far from the desert
And in no way disconcerted:
Because I am swallowed
By the smallest oasis –
Which stretched open, yawning,
Its sweet mouth,
The most sweetly-scented little mouth –
And I fell in,
Down, right the way through – and landed
Among you, dearest maidens! Selah.

Hail to that whale
If it welcomed
Its guests like this! – (Do you understand
My learned allusion here) –
Hail to his belly
If his belly was
An oasis as sweet as this:
But this I call into question –
Since I come from Europe,
Which is more sceptical
Than a fussy old maid.
May God improve it!
Amen!

Here I sit
In this smallest oasis,

Scorched like a date,
Brown, sweet, oozing golden juice,
Aching for a girl's pouting mouth,
But longing even more for girlish,
Ice-cold, snow-white, biting
Teeth: the hearts of all burning dates
Lust after these. Selah.

Like, too much like
That aforementioned southern fruit,
I lie here,
Sniffed-out and circled
By little flying insects,
And also by smaller
More foolish and sinful
Desires and ideas –
Surrounded by you,
Silent kitten-girls,
And spilling-out scruples,
Dudu and Suleika,
Sphinxed around, so that I may stuff
A great deal of feeling into two words:
(God forgive me for
This sin of speech!....)
Here I sit sniffing the cleanest air;
Truly, the air of Paradise,
Bright, drifting air, streaked with gold,
As fresh as any air that ever
Fell from the moon –
Did it come by chance,
Or was it from lustfulness,
As the old poets say?
But I, the doubter, call all this into question;
Since I come from Europe,
Which is more sceptical than

A fussy old maid.
May God improve it!
Amen.

Gulping down the finest air,
Nostrils opened-out like goblets,
Without future, without memory,
I sit here among you,
Dearest maidens,
Looking at a palm tree
And watching how, like a dancer,
It bends and sways, and wriggles its hips,
– If you watch it long enough you do it yourself!
Like a dancer who, it seems,
Has stood too long, too dangerously long,
On one skinny leg –
So she has forgotten
Her other leg?
At least I, alas, in vain,
Sought the missing
Twin jewel
– The other leg, of course –
In the sacred locale
Of her dear, dainty
Little fluttering, flowing, fan-wafting skirt.
If you would believe me,
You sweetest of girls, I tell you:
She has lost it!
It has gone!
Gone forever!
That poor other leg!
Isn't it a shame about that other leg!
Where could it be now, abandoned and sad?
Shaking with fear before an
Angry, blonde

Lion-monster? Or chewed off, perhaps,
Broken to bits –
Pitiable, alas! Broken to bits! Selah.

But do not weep,
You gentle hearts!
Do not weep, you
Date-hearts! Milky breasts!
You sweetwood treasure
Chests of the heart!
Do not weep,
Pale Dudu!
Courage, Suleika! Be a man!
Or would a few uplifting words
Be appropriate here?
An anointed proverb?
Or a solemn prayer?
Ahem! Rise up, dignity!
Virtuous European dignity!
Blow, blow up again,
Bellows of virtue,
And roar!
Roar morally!
Roar like a lion of morality
Before the daughters of the desert!
For you see, dear girls,
Virtuous howling
Is loved above all else
By European passion, European taste!
And since I stand here,
As a European,
I can do nothing else, so help me God!
Amen!

Deserts grow: woe to him who harbours deserts! [DD]

www.creationbooks.com